Tissington Village

Published by:
Derbyshire County Council, Libraries and Heritage Department,
County Hall, Matlock, Derbyshire DE4 3AG

Edited by:
Jenny Edgar, Literature Development Officer, Derbyshire County Council, with Cynthia and Geoff Buckley, Hubert Doxey, Ken Harwood, Andy Pollock, Alan Rimmer.

Photographs:
Nigel Tissington - Colour Portraits and Back Cover
J. H. Bentley - Small B/W on Front Cover
Clare Willmer
Derby Evening Telegraph - Derby Advertiser

Cover Design:
Trains and Trails Group

Printed by:
F M Repro Limited, Liversedge, West Yorkshire. Tel. 01924 411011

ISBN: 0 9034636 9 5

CONTENTS

CONTRIBUTORS

Jean Bailey
Dr. Barnett
Fred Birch
Tony Broome
Edward Buckley
Cynthia Buckley
Geoff Buckley
Chris Coombs
Susan Davis
Hubert Doxey MBE
Huw Edwards
Steve Farren
Dave Gregory
Bill Hallows
Keith Hallows
Ken Harwood
Maria Harwood
Tony Holmes
Susan Howard
Robin Jeffcoat
Rick Jillings
Geoff Kirk
Mary Maxwell
Hilda Mellor
George O'Shaughnessy
Ken Parker
Eric Plumtree
Andy Pollock
Bill Richardson
Ron Riley
Alan Rimmer
Jenny Scurfield
Herbert Sheppard
Gertie Shipley
May Smith
Trevor Steed
Meg Tarlton
Ian Taylor
Derrick Wain
Glynn Waite
Ken Watson
J.W. Whitehead
Pat Winder
Phyllis Wragg
Trevor Wragg

The Trains and Trails Group was saddened by the sudden deaths of Bill Hallows, who had been an enthusiastic and involved member of the group, and Graham Wain who accompanied his brother Derrick to several meetings. Thanks go to Bill's widow, Betty, who has agreed that his work could be included in the book.

The Trains and Trails Group would like to thank the following people:

The Countryside Service and Libraries and Heritage Departments of Derbyshire County Council, the Peak District National Park Authority, the Peak District Interpretation Project, the Derbyshire Dales District Council and the Local Heritage Initiative Fund for their interest and support in the project.

Special thanks to Carolyn Luscombe for her work with the group and Ed Mollon for his help with the project.

FOREWORD

From the beginning of the railway age people have been fascinated by railways. For the many enthusiasts there are books by the score giving details of engines, tracks, signals; everything to do with the physical aspects of running a complex travel service.

However, that is only one side of the story. We can only begin to imagine the impact of such an innovative industry coming to rural Derbyshire particularly as it was originally intended to be a canal. In October 1810 plans were afoot to join the Peak Forest Canal, that had opened in 1800, with the Cromford Canal at an estimated cost of £650,000. Then came a major obstacle; there would be insufficient water at the summit level. Undeterred, Josias Jessop, the engineer, drew up plans for a railway basing them on the same principles used in constructing canals. Josias died one year after the railway was begun and the work was completed by Thomas Woodhouse. The railway was built with long level sections connected by rope-worked inclines, similar in design to the locks of a canal. The tracks began at Cromford, 278 feet above sea level, and at their highest point, Ladmanlow, were 1264 feet above sea level. Several different engines would have been used to climb the one thousand feet over the fifteen and a half miles of track to the summit.

The Cromford and High Peak railway was opened in 1830-1831 and the Tissington Railway in 1899 with both lines offering employment in the area and a means for people living in rural villages to reach towns that had previously only been reached by a long journey on horse-back or on foot.

The industry affected everyone whether they lived in a town or in the country and, whenever people are affected by change, there are stories to be told. This book tells the stories that have been handed down through generations and of the men who worked for the railways throughout their lives with a loyalty that is difficult to imagine in the twenty-first century. They tell of village girls circling the duck pond, hoping to catch a glimpse of the newly employed railwaymen. Those girls and their relatives may well have rolled milk churns to the station, churns that were destined for large towns and cities that the youngsters had never visited. Perhaps they never did.

When the end of the small railways came it brought sadness to many who had been involved with the industry. The Cromford and High Peak Railway finally closed in 1967 to the regret of those who had worked on it. Thankfully the railway tracks and buildings have not been left to deteriorate but have undergone yet another change. Before the closure of the lines Derbyshire County Council and the Peak Park Planning Board began negotiations with the British Railways Board to buy the Cromford and High Peak and the Ashbourne to Buxton railways. Their intention was to develop them into a route for walking and pony trekking. The sleepers were removed, often being bought to use as edging for garden paths and flowerbeds, and the metal rails were taken to be re-used or sold as scrap.

Where there were tracks there are now trails, opening the countryside to people who come from cities, towns and villages to walk and cycle on the High Peak and Tissington Trails. Starting at Cromford, the High Peak Trail is joined by the Tissington Trail at Parsley Hay, north of Newhaven and finishes in the Peak District National Park near Chelmorton.

In yet another collaboration Derbyshire County Council and the Peak District National Park's Countryside Service decided that the stories of the people of the railways and trails should be told. In this book you will meet people who worked on the line, villagers who used the railway to travel to school, others who went away to war and returned to the peacefulness of their home only to find it difficult to settle down to a village pace of life after their years in action. There are the walkers and cyclists, who come from the cities and towns to wander through the Derbyshire countryside, who describe just what the trails mean to them and the rangers and wardens who continue to ensure the trails remain a special part of our environment.

Each person who has contributed to this book, whatever their connection with the railways and the trails, retains a memory of the tracks and trails heritage that is uniquely theirs.

Jenny Edgar
Literature Development Officer
Derbyshire County Council
2001

Duckpond at Hartington

LIFE IN THE VILLAGES

The Cromford and High Peak and the Ashbourne to Buxton Railways ran through some of the most beautiful countryside in Britain. Spaced out amongst fields and woodlands are the towns and villages of Derbyshire; Cromford with its mill pond and water wheel; Ashbourne that is still a flourishing market town; Hartington, famous for its Stilton cheese and Tissington, with seven wells that are dressed each year, attract visitors from all over Britain and from abroad.

The people who live and work in these places have seen changes and recognised the need to move with the times whilst managing to retain much of the quality of life that was enjoyed in the early 1900's. Some people have only ever lived in one village. Others moved into Derbyshire to find work on the railways and stayed and all of them, locals or incomers, regard their part of Derbyshire with great affection.

Tissington was a lovely place to grow up. We didn't need to leave the village to have some fun. People came to us. The Etches used to bring the stallion to serve the mares. He'd be all dressed up, red, white and blue ribbons down his mane and tail and bells on his harness. He'd arrive at the station in a railway horse-box with a fellow with him who was dressed in leather leggings to keep his trousers clean. They came to Tissington first then on to Thorpe, Parwich and all around then back they'd come to the station. I used to think how marvellous it all looked but I daren't go too near.

There was an old fellow from the Potteries who came by train to Ashbourne but goodness knows how he managed. He carried a big clothes-basket on his head full of pots and pans, plates, dishes, that type of thing. After he'd finished here he'd walk across to Thorpe and

Tissington Village

Parwich with his basket of pots on his head. Then he'd come back by Alsop and catch a train there. Years and years he came. We always used to buy something off him, poor chap.

Then there was Old Dodger, the tinker, who used to push my old pram around. He sold lace, elastic, buttons, cottons, all sorts of stuff. The village shop sold all those things but we still used to buy from him. And I worked at the shop! One year he brought his little dog that had a curly tail over its back. Our cat had just had kittens and this dog ran round, saw the cat and went towards her. Our Topsy - she was a beggar when she'd got kittens - jumped on his back and they went round and round that shed and our toilet about twenty times. Dodger was shouting 'Call your cat off my dog – she'll kill him!'

Every year there was a Harvest Festival Auction when we all gave what we could the week before and then bought it back again! Me and Jack Harvey used to love to buy a jelly. We'd split it up and eat it before we got home.

Children went to small village schools but once they reached secondary education age some of them went out of the villages to the town and the railway really made a difference.

There were between twenty and thirty children and two teachers, a Miss Gold and a Miss Smith, who both lived in the village.

Later, when Mrs Willescroft was teaching, we'd skip off school if we knew the hounds were going to be out and follow them right down to Bradbourn Brook. Of course we'd be back late for school and she used a skipping rope across my legs. Ooh! I knew she had done as well.

When I told my dad he just said 'Well, you shouldn't have gone'. I'd be about eight or nine, I suppose. I just wanted to see what was going on.

The infants were five to eight years old and the Seniors were older children who hadn't passed to go to the Grammar School. They stayed on at Tissington until they were fourteen. There were quite a few of us went to Queen Elizabeth's Grammar School in Ashbourne. There were two lads who used to walk across the fields from Parwich to catch the train from here. It didn't take them long, it's only a couple of miles, but they'd have the same to do at night.

I was lucky because I got into the Grammar School for free. My parents didn't have to pay fees or the train fares. Some people, the ones who didn't quite make it, got what they called a free place that was half-and-half. I suppose they had to pay something. But you had to be really good to get the free place. In my particular year there were three of us, Mr. Mellor and his sister and me.

Most of the older children used the train to get to school. When the train stopped under the bridge to fill up with water the boys used to spit over the bridge at the firemen. Not to be outdone these firemen would let the engine back a bit and go 'Shppt' and let all black soot go and the lads would be covered in it.

Saturday night was dance night. The highlight of the week.

Sixpenny hops with Miss Smith, one of the schoolteachers, playing piano. Round and round we'd go, dancing the Valetta, the Two Step, the Barn Dance and the St. Bernard's Waltz. By the time we were finished we were parched but there were no refreshments, no matter how long we'd been dancing.

'I'm Burlington Bertie from Bow' – that was Jimmy Walker with his beard and his stick. He used to have us roaring with laughter.

Nowhere can better Tissington when it comes to the Derbyshire tradition of well dressing.

My grandfather used to dress the Hall Well with its border of castles and in later years I took over, putting the flower petals in. The tradition started as a way of giving thanks for pure water. At the time of the Black Death it was the only water that was safe to drink so the villagers had a lot to be grateful for.

Welldressing
preparation

Before water was piped into the cottages every bit had to be fetched for drinking, washing, everything. Later there were ordinary taps outside the cottage. Not that we used them for everything because we caught water off the roof into a water butt and it was smashing for the washing, boiled up in a copper but our drinking water came from a tap and because it was spring water we didn't have to boil it.

The pretty village and the ritual dressing of the wells attracted people from miles around, as it still does.

When the trains were running visitors would come from Manchester and stay for a week. My grandparents used to do bed and breakfast for them, taking a family of four then perhaps another couple of people. It was a way of supplementing their income during the war. My granny had five daughters; one stopped at home, one worked at the vicarage, one at the schoolhouse, and another at the hall. When my mother was a girl she used to deliver telegrams to Alstonfield and she'd just get back into the house and there'd be another one waiting and she had to go back again. She used to bike seven miles there and seven back, all for the grand sum of sixpence. The old dog used to follow her because there was no traffic in those days. He'd have the telegram in his mouth and my mother was nearly out of her mind because she thought they'd never be able to read it.

You didn't wait until you were grown up to earn your keep. Childhood meant school and work. I was eleven when I started working on the farm. Each night my job was to shut the hens up in their coop. We didn't dare leave them out because the fox would have them. It was my job to make sure they were let out again in the morning but I couldn't always do it because it wasn't light enough. The wood on the roof of the hen coop was a bit rotten and one night the clever fox found a way in. By this time we were down to six hens and he took the lot of them.

When we let our ducks out they'd all waddle down to the village pond. They'd come back at night, as good as gold, to be shut in.

When I was a bit older I ploughed fields with a horse-drawn plough, dug turnips and joined in the haymaking. This was all done in the evenings because we couldn't have time off school to do it. The men'd sort it during the day then we'd do whatever was needed when we got home. Potato picking, things like that. Milking cows was done by hand then, right through to the late forties when the machines were invented but we didn't get ours until 1959. I never reckoned much to milking but I had to do it.

Later on I worked at the village shop, just until I got married. We used to sell everything. Mrs Twigg was a regular caller.

'Don't let me forget my Carter's Little Liver Pills, will you?'

I don't really know what they were for even though I've sold dozens of them.

And there were Beechams Pills in little round boxes. My granddad used to take those almost every night and Uncle Willie used to pop one in his mouth then have a spoonful of jam to take the taste away.

We sold no end of bread that we bought in from Staffords. The Swindells family used to have eight two pound loaves on a Wednesday and again on a Saturday. Stafford'd bring sacks, proper sacks that they used for corn that his mother had washed clean, and he'd put the bread in, throw the sack over his shoulder and set off for Drakelow.

Before about 1930 the farmers had to sign an agreement to sell the milk. There was no Milk-Marketing Board then. The railway made a big difference because milk could be sold farther afield.

When I was helping my dad we brought milk down in a horse and cart. My job was to pick up the churns at the farm and bring them down using Dolly, the old mare, and a trap. You couldn't see the railway-bridge for smoke but Dolly never bothered because she was so used to the trains going by her field.

There was a down side to village life, particularly when the majority of people were farming.

T.B. testing of cattle came in during the fifties. If the animals reacted to the vaccination we had to get rid of them. It happened round here quite a bit and it took a while for the farmers to get it clear.

That was at the time they were still checking children, doing the mass x-rays in the towns. If the test came up you were either immune or you'd got it. Fenny Bentley was hit badly. There were a number of one up, one down houses with nine or more living in them. The people weren't poor enough to starve but the water came from a tap that was always breaking and contaminating the water. That was in the late 40's. They use to object to paying rates when they didn't have any sewage facilities so they took the buckets out from the toilets and tipped them into the brook. It's only been in the last fifteen years that Fenny Bentley has had mains sewerage. That's the other side to country living!

Just like Tissington the village of Hartington had families who had lived there for many years.

My mother's family were the Shirleys' and they go back at least four generations. They lived at 'Sprink Farm' up towards Pilsbury. My father's side, the Rileys', came from Warslow and my great-great grandfather lived at Stoneyfold Farm. I was born in the village and we lived up the dale in a tiny cottage. There were children all the way down the dale - families of eight or ten were not unusual. Of course they all played out and they'd shout 'Motor! Motor!' and we'd all run out just to see a motor car go past. In those days there wasn't a square inch of tarmac in Hartington, just a dusty dirt road and when a motor came there was dust for half-an-hour after it had gone by.

Not that there were many cars around. Doctor Twigg had a motor-bike with a wicker-basket side-chair and the Bateman family, at Hartington Hall, had a big, six cylinder Napier. It used to fill the road. The driver of the Model 'T' Ford at the Charles Cotton Hotel was my

The Dale at Hartington

grandfather's brother. He used to fetch people from Hartington Station and he'd keep shouting 'Gee up, Gee up,' as though the car was a horse.

We couldn't go out on trips because we didn't have cars but I'd got my brother and sisters at home and I suppose we just played ordinary games. There were special days like Shrove Tuesday. It was called 'Whip and Top Day' and we were given a half-day holiday. Whilst we whipped the tops down the street as fast as we could the girls played shuttlecock.

Alcock's Drapers bought in whips and tops specially for that day and sold them at a penny a whip, a penny a top. One lad, Ted Bates, saved up for weeks so that he'd have two pennies and he rushed in to the shop to buy this whip and top. He'd got them at long last, ran out of the shop and was so anxious to try it he put the top down and whipped it straight back through the shop window. It took him a long time to save up enough pennies for a new window.

Once a year there was a Beef Fair in the village where villagers bought their meat for Wakes Week. We made a lot of fuss about Wakes Week – it was a real holiday. The village was packed full of amusements. There were steam- driven roundabouts, coconut shies, swing boats and a roll of pennies. You couldn't see the front of the Devonshire Arms for stalls.

The Stilton cheese industry was brought to Hartington by a Mr. J.M. Nuttall who lived at Dove Cottage and the cheese company is still known as J.M. Nuttall and Co. He and his wife had no children and there was a family named Burton who were fairground people from Ashbourne who always came for the Wakes Week. They were a rough lot with about a dozen kids. He was a right beery old fella and she seemed as rough as a gipsy, perhaps worse and they'd got all these dirty little kids running about.

One year Mr Nuttall went to see their mother to tell her he'd taken a fancy to one of the lads and asked if he could sort of adopt it and bring it up.

'I know you can't make a hasty decision,' he said. 'I'll come and see you at the end of the week.'

Sure enough he went back at the end of the week and the woman said 'You can't have any of my children but I'll lend you the old man'. I mean, what bigger insult can you give a man?

There were all sorts of stories handed down. Like the one about Bob Oliver, who was landlord at the Devonshire. A customer of his lived on her own just across the road from him. One Sunday night the old woman was getting a bit down in the dumps, a bit old and nobody bothering with her. Over she went to talk to Bob Oliver and told him her woes.Bob says 'Never mind, missus. There's many a good tune played on an old fiddle.'

The old lady said 'Aye, but it's getting someone to play it!'

In my grandparents time there was a man who used to stay at the Charles Cotton Hotel. Only problem was this chap kept flying off the handle so they farmed him out down in the village. Every so often this man'd cause a panic amongst the village folk and the only one who could quieten him was my grandfather, a rough old farmer type.

On one occasion this man went off the rails altogether and somebody came out from Ashbourne to certify him. Grandfather was called to take him to Cheddleton Mental Asylum and he collared this little chap who was making such a fuss and he went as quiet as a lamb. A dapper little fella, all dressed up. Granddad gets his horse and cart and puts the poor chap in it and off they go.

Well – my grandfather was very rough at the best of times. This particular day he'd hurt his foot and you know those little shovels for stoking the boiler? The ones with a small handle? He'd put one of those on his foot because he couldn't get his boot on. Tied this shovel on.

The journey was uneventful until they reached the asylum doors. As soon as he got inside this quiet man who had been certified says 'I've brought this man in for you,' pointing at my grandfather who was dressed in his old working clothes with a copper shovel tied to one foot. Granddad blustered and carried on but he'd one hell of a job getting away.

Everybody talks about the weather but round here..! The winters – well, snow everywhere. We've heard tell of how there were Arctic conditions between Longcliffe and Buxton in 1895. The snow-clearers were covered in snow that froze to their clothes and they ended up with frostbite. They pushed straw inside their clothes for a bit of insulation. As fast as the tracks and tunnels were cleared the wind blew the snow straight back in.

1880 had been another bad one. The really exposed areas of the High Peak had drifts of ten to twelve feet. People had to tunnel their way out of their homes. The roads were blocked and the quarries closed down but the railway workers carried on working, shifting snow from tracks and tunnels.

We've had some pretty bad 'uns more recently. In the early forties we couldn't get down Station Road on foot so we borrowed some sledges and sledged down to try and get some bread from the bakehouse. The baker gave us two loaves to share between four houses. Luckily he'd got a good stock of flour or else there'd have been no bread for anyone. Not that it was much good when he ran out of yeast. Somebody had to walk to Youlgreave from Friden, ploughing through the snow just to get this little bag of yeast.

But for the worst ever winter that I remember it has to be the nineteen-forty-seven snow.

I'd just finished in the Marines when the snow came. Talk about feeling trapped. There I was, a young chap who'd just been round the world, up in the Arctic, all over the place, coming home to a place like Hartington, especially when we got trapped in for six weeks. I've never settled since. Not properly.

Ron Riley

Hartington Church

Another well known family goes back for seven generations.

We had a beautiful home - Hyde Lane Farm- that was a small-holding just half-a-mile out of the village and that's where I was born in 1909. I lived there all my life except for these last two years. Even when I married, my husband and I went to live at home with my father and mother.

Granddad was Mark Greatbach, a miller, who came to work at Hartington at the 'Miller of the Dove'. He'd come from Werrington where his family lived in a public house. They had a working windmill and they can be dangerous things. Granddad's brother was killed by one of the sails. Granddad was a Methodist and always took me to the Chapel at Hall Bank in the village. The seats were much too high for me - I was only little - so he'd lift me up to stand on them.

I was five when the First World War broke out and when a Zeppelin airship went over we did what we always did in a thunderstorm; my mother bundled us up and we'd go to my grandma's in the village. I don't know why it felt safe there, but it did. When I was at school we always came down to my grandma's in the village and had dinner with her.

When there was snow, and there often was, we used to sledge down to school. There were no cars, you see. No nothing. That meant we could play in the roads and the games were different to what they are now - hopscotch, skipping, that type of thing. And church was very important, a service in the morning and Sunday school at night.

I never liked school. My sister was the clever one, not me. We used to do reading, writing, arithmetic and home-management, sewing and all that. I was glad when I could leave. It meant I could work on the smallholding.

When we'd grown up a bit my sister and I were sometimes allowed to go to a dance at the Village Hall. We didn't even have a wireless at home. Some of my friends used to ask us how we could live without a radio but my dad played piano and we'd stand around singing and my sister, my father and I were in the choir. And we'd play cards and ring-ball. Come winter-time we cut old clothes into strips and made peg hearth rugs. Somewhere at home there's still the peg I used to use. Oh yes, we had entertainment.

My husband was born and bred in the village too. I'd known him all my life then one year at the Wakes he walked me home. That was the start of it and I was just seventeen. We didn't marry until I was twenty-five and then we wasted a lot of time. We didn't have our son for another three-and-a-half years.

My husband and my father went out to work and I did all the farming. It was heavy work even though it was only a smallholding because there wasn't enough money to pay for the farm implements we needed so it was all done by hand. We had cows and pigs but the pigs were really a lot of trouble. When they farrowed we used to have to sit up with them. I've farrowed many a pig, I have.

I loved farming, haymaking and getting up a field full of turnips and our own potatoes. Oh, the first crop of potatoes out of the garden – there's nothing quite like it.

We'd got our son when the bad winter of 1947 came. The lane was completely blocked and the snow was level across the top of the walls. My husband and father used to carry coal up when the coal merchants had left it in the village.

Being cut off didn't bother us much because we'd kill a pig and there'd be two sides of bacon hanging up and a few hams. We'd eggs from the hens and our own milk and bread and butter. My mother was always one to provide-in for winter and I always have done so since. With a well-stocked store cupboard you knew it was there and the family wouldn't go without.

Gertie Shipley

Hartington Hall

The Sunday School outing was an important part of village life.

We'd hop on the train and head out to Belle Vue in Manchester. Our parents came with us and we took our picnics along. My mum used to make Eiffel Tower Lemonade from lemonade crystals and boiling water, then she'd top it up with cold water out of the spring. We took home-made cakes and paste, salmon or egg sandwiches. It seemed to take a long time to get to Belle Vue but it was worth it to see the man on the motor bike that rode the wall of death. He'd start at the bottom and spiral up and up so that he looked as if he was stuck on the side of the wall.

Not everyone had such memorable outings.

'It was our Sunday School treat and we walked to Hulme End in the Leek and Manifold Valley, got on the train, went about six miles down the track to Beeston Tor, came back to Hulme End and walked back home again. That was it. But if I hadn't gone I'd never have had a ride on the train.'

Like Tissington, Hartington had its own dance nights and the teenagers were able to enjoy a different type of music when Derrick Wain and his work mates came to the village hall.

I was working in a joiner's shop and there were a few of us who played instruments. Inevitably we were christened 'The Splinters.' I can't read a note of music but I can play instruments. I was on mandolin and banjo. The bloke playing bass hadn't an inkling about music but he got himself an old tea chest, painted it like a domino and made a one-string bass. The guy who played drums, he'd get up and dance to see what type of rhythm he had to play!

It snowballed. We began by doing concerts for old people and found ourselves an agent. We came to Hartington Village Hall once a month for six years and did we have some nights! A coach-load of people would come with us and I've seen that place seething. We had a smashing time playing all the old stuff, the sing-along. We even played with the Beatles when they came to Buxton.

One year we were asked to play at the wedding of the winner of the Miss Derbyshire competition. Her mother and father were Hungarian and the guests came from all over the world.

We all went to her house in Winster and everyone lined up, the groom, the vicar and her guests. Her dress was absolutely smothered in money. I'd never seen that before. Everyone who was Hungarian was in their national costume and we paraded through the village and turned into the church. The only thing they wanted us to play was 'She loves you, yeh, yeh, yeh' by the Beatles! So we played that all the way. When we came out of the church there was a beautiful stage- coach with six horses waiting to take the bride and groom to Darley Dale Institute for the reception. We paraded them back to the village, piled our instruments into our cars, a Police escort came with us and we drove like the clappers to get set up on the steps of the Institute. 'She loves you, yeh, yeh, yeh' again and again.

We played till nine o'clock that night then about twenty coaches turned up and took us all to the Bath Hotel at Matlock where the bride's mother worked. We played all night until breakfast time at eight-fifteen and we didn't repeat ourselves once!

There's no fun like playing in a band.

Derrick Wain

When they first opened the Palace Hotel in Buxton, at twelve noon on the 6th of June 1868, the people in the village wanted to know all about it. One of the men in the village had been to see it and when he came home a big crowd gathered round him.

'Tell us what it's like, this marvellous new hotel.'

'Eh,' he said,' there were that many in for lunch they had two men mixing mustard with grafting spades in the back yard.'

The Hartington Cheese Factory is famous world-wide for its Stilton cheese and for well over a century it has been at the forefront of cheese making.

In 1878 the village won the twenty pound first prize for developing a cheese-making machine. That was a lot of money. This was an early cheese vat and held about two hundred gallons. The machine was filled with milk and there was a steam pipe running round the inside, sort of a double jacket. There wasn't stainless steel in those days, it was tin over steel and the outside was cast iron. Round the inside was a coil of steam pipes where they could turn the steam on from a boiler and get that up to the temperature they needed for cheese making. Of course they got condensation inside that would run out of the bottom and they'd use the tap to run the whey out of the vat when the curds solidified. First of all the whey went for pig feed but later on it was sold as dried powder for cosmetics and biscuits. They still use it in biscuits and sometimes I can still taste it.

Strangely enough we might never have had the Stilton Cheese Factory here if it hadn't been for an outbreak of Foot and Mouth Disease. The Nuttall family had a cheese factory in Leicestershire making Stilton on the home farm. The outbreak of Foot and Mouth put them more or less out of business. That's why they came to Hartington.

Foot and Mouth hit people round here pretty hard too. It was everywhere and it ruined some farmers. Our neighbours next door and across the road had to have all their cattle put down. My father died in

January 1968 as we were just about at the end of the Foot and Mouth epidemic. We'd blocked the drive with a gate to stop anybody coming in but we had to take it down for the Doctor to get through. Even though it was nearly over we still had to take precautions. Disinfectant and such like.

People earned their livings at all sorts of trades and often had two or three jobs to keep the family going.

Our family did a bit of anything including undertaking. It's all in my grandfather's cash book. I've kept it all these years. 'One child's coffin, three pounds ten shillings.' That's three pounds fifty pence. 'All oak, lined with domett cotton wadding for a shroud.' That child was three days old. There were any amount of infant deaths in those days.

When anybody died it was unthinkable for them not to be put upstairs or in the front room. They lay there for two or three days and we dressed them up in this domett and made them look well. People are the poorer for the change. You need to say goodbye to people and in your own house is where to do it.

That isn't the only change of practice when there is a death in the family.

My daughter found the funeral card for one of my children. She'd never seen one before. Years ago they always had a black-edged card and envelope. There was always a verse inside the card and my Dad had made up the verse for my son's card.

My son was seven-and-a-half months when he died. He had spina-bifida and there was nothing they could do. Maybe nowadays it would have been different because he was a bright little chap.

The idyllic village life that many town dwellers dreamt of had an ingredient that they might have found stifling. The feudal system, even now, is alive and well in many villages, including Tissington.

Tissington still belongs to the FitzHerberts, all the cottages belong to Sir Richard. There'd been quite a lot of freeholders in Tissington right up to the middle of the nineteenth century but about 1919 the FitzHerberts started buying everything under the sun and they expanded out into Bentley. Most of Fenny Bentley's been re-sold now.

There's an unbelievable amount of estate papers. At one time it was the single largest deposit in the Derbyshire Archives.

Everybody in Tissington lives here on a rented basis, all except one farmer whose ancestors managed to keep hold of his farm. The only houses that have been sold are the railway cottages. The Council bought them from the Railway and they were rented until the tenants were able to buy them. The railway workers who lived in them when the railway closed were able to stay. No one threw them out.

There were things that barred you from getting an estate cottage. Years ago, if you didn't go to church - that was enough. When they heard of new workmen coming it was a case of 'Do they go to church? No? Ah, well. Doubt if we'll want them then.'

My Dad was a gardener at Tissington Hall. When I was born in 1920 he was living at Sycamore House with my mother, grandmother and granddad. There were eight of us altogether and it was too crowded. When I arrived on the scene they decided to look for somewhere and Dad asked the agent about getting a cottage.

The agent said 'We can't find cottages for railway men.'

'I'm not on the railway now. I've been finished because they're cutting down,' my Dad told him.

'There's houses for anyone who's in work on the estate,' said the agent so Dad signed up for the estate and we got a cottage. There was a big vegetable garden at the Hall and they needed no end of gardeners. It was all dug by spade, double dug with proper manure from their own farms. Dad took over from the head gardener when he retired. He didn't really want to do it but Sir William asked him to - so he did. That's how it was then.

Town Well, Tissington

Steam in the hills

THE SNORTING HORSES

Many people have fond memories of the railways and how their lives were improved by the engines rattling through their villages but for those who actually worked with the 'Snorting Horses' there was an important additional aspect; a security of employment that was highly valued. The railway people, sometimes several from the same family, had a pride in their work and a strong sense of comradeship. A tradition had begun.

There were that many of them that we called it the 'Cope and Allen' line! Mr. Cope was the station-master in Tissington and a Mr. Allen was the station-master at Alsop and there was another at Thorpe. My great-uncle, who lived in Tissington village was an Allen who had been on the line for a long time. He was a signalman and a keen gardener and he built a rockery at the signalbox where he grew masses of flower round it. Marigolds, delphiniums, real cottage garden plants.

If father drove an engine his son wanted to go one better. A natural progression.

'How would you like to work on the railway?' I was already in work as a painter but I said I'd think about it. Dad had a word with the shed foreman, or, to give him his official title, the Motive Power Superintendent, who said there was an opening for me if I wanted it. Providing I came up to scratch, of course.

I was seventeen when I started as a cleaner in 1947 and I loved it. I was still in that job when I was called up for The Forces. I came back after two years to find they'd counted all the trips I would have done if I'd stayed. Three hundred and thirteen trips amounted to one increment in the pay scale. Show me a job where that would happen today.

My son works the railways now and my father is an ex-railway worker. My grandfather, who was killed in the First World War, started as a young lad and my great-grandfather worked the railways too.

The Hallows family with a recorded span of 160 years service provides a not untypical example of long service.

The tradition of 'following in father's footsteps' was common in all types of work, whether tilling the soil on a farm or taking a job in the pits. What was good enough for father was good enough for his sons; but the railways were somehow different. The sons still took up a post with the railways but not because there was no alternative. For most young men the loyalty which their fathers felt towards their employers and to the actual work on the railways were the deciding factors.

The Hallows family certainly viewed their work in this way. From 1834 to the present day there have been Hallows associated with the Cromford and High Peak Railway and our family story, not always a happy one, began with the birth of Sam Hallows, born in 1806. In the 1841 census he was described as a bookkeeper for the CHPR at Parsley Hay. In later documents he is usually described as a wharfinger – a man who manages a wharf - and he also sold coal, whether on behalf of a contractor or as his own sideline isn't clear. Like the majority of families he had a large brood, fathering twelve children by his first wife, Hannah. No less than six of his sons found employment with the railway company.

Ralph, born in 1829, was Samuel's eldest son and worked as a driver of fly wagons. On the 9th October 1854 he was the driver of a train that was on its way from Whaley Bridge to Cromford. The train broke free on the Middleton Incline and crashed into some stone wagons. Ralph died within a few hours.

Samuel had a double loss in that year when his wife, Hannah, also died. No doubt originally united in mourning Ralph's young widow

Celia and Samuel married in 1858 and Samuel fathered two more children in this second marriage. Family members must have had some enjoyment working out their relationships after that!

Samuel's second son was John, born in 1831, who took over at Parsley Hay when his father died in 1863. At the time of his death in 1887 he was Stationmaster, having worked his way up through the ranks.

The third son, William, began working at Sheep Pasture Incline in 1836 before moving to Middleton where he and his family lived in the railway house. Whilst working as an incline pulley-man William had an accident that resulted in him having a leg amputated. Despite his disability the company held his job open for him and when he recovered he returned to work until his retirement in 1904.

Joseph was the next Hallows to join the railway as a labourer. Sadly whilst working in Hopton Tunnel in 1880, blasting the stone to enlarge the roof, he and two work colleagues were killed by falling stone.

Young Samuel, born in 1845, was at first a labourer living at Monyash but by 1876 he was living with his family in the railway house at Hopton Top and his occupation was described as engine tester.

There was yet more tragedy for the family when James, born in 1849, was killed at the age of twenty-six by a wagon running over him on Hopton Incline.

In the years from 1834 to 1875 the Hallows family had suffered four deaths associated with the railways and one serious accident.

Young Samuel had fathered seven children, all sons, and it was Herbert, his youngest son who was born in 1878, who carried on the family tradition of working on the railways, completing forty-five years of service, thirty of those as an engine-man. A strong union man, he was awarded a disablement grant of thirty pounds by the NUR at a presentation at the Rising Sun in Middleton. According to the speech given that day 'the men had come to respect Brother Hallows with almost a sense of worship'.

Herbert had a large family of thirteen children, nine of whom were daughters and only one of his sons, his namesake, followed him into railway work. Herbert Junior completed thirty years of service with the railway.

It would be reasonable to assume that with the closure of the railway the link with the Hallows family would come to an end but, when the tracks were superseded by long-distance paths, yet another member of the Hallows family began work. Bill Hallows, the son of Herbert Junior, worked at the Cycle Hire Department at Middleton Top. It is nearly two hundred years since Samuel, the first Hallows railwayman, was born and, in one way or another, the Hallows family have been connected to the railway ever since.

Bill and Keith Hallows with help from others.

The Wibberley family's connections with the railway began before the First World War when Thomas worked the Ashbourne to Buxton line and his wife, Lizzie, was midwife in Fenny Bentley, the village where they and their six children lived. Their youngest daughter, Hilda, remembers Thomas returning from war and taking up normal life again.

I was born on 21st April, 1914 and I didn't have time to get to know my father because he was called up to the Great War. Mother was left with six children, all of them at school except myself.

She coped all right but when he came home in 1918 I didn't know him. He soon got round me and was a wonderful father to us all even though he was very strict. Before long someone from the railway told him there was a job vacant on the High Peak Railway and a cottage too. He went to have a look around, found out what work he'd have to do and accepted it.

My brother worked on a farm and my father asked the farmer if he could borrow a horse and cart to do the flitting from Fenny Bentley to the new cottage. I don't know how many loads we had but my mother set off early with me in a pushchair to walk the eight or nine miles. When we got to Alsop Moor she saw a pony and trap coming and the driver stopped and offered us a lift. He took us as far as Biggin Lane End. We were very grateful to him because it meant we'd only another three miles to walk. By the time we got there they were busy unloading the first load from the cart.

There wasn't any piped water at the cottage but the engine drivers were very good and brought us spring water and we used water that we'd collected off the house for cleaning and washing clothes.

Father made two lovely gardens near the house and two more each side of the railway line. We always had enough vegetables to last the winter and gooseberries, raspberries, blackcurrants and strawberries for jam. The farmers around about let us have some fields to put hens on. That was a big help because we could sell some of the eggs.

Dad's new job meant he had to walk the full length of the line from Friden to Longcliffe once every day to make sure everything was in order for the trains the next day. He would take a few keys and a hammer with him in case he needed them, especially round Gotham Curve. Mother was given the job of opening the crossing gates and trimming the paraffin lamps on the top of them when they had to be used in winter time. For that she got half-a-crown a week.

It's a good job we were all used to walking because when I started at Biggin school, when I was five, I had to walk it. If I got wet, and I often did, I had to dry off round a stove in the middle of the room.

When I was eleven my parents bought me an old bicycle which made the journey a lot quicker. I left school when I was fourteen and got a job on a farm not far away with a farmer and his mother. That meant we were all out earning our livings. I've never wanted to move away and when I married my husband we settled at Pike Hall. I've been here ever since.

Hilda Mellor

From Alan Rimmer Collection

Parents and sister of Hilda Mellor

Another family who figure strongly in the story of the railways is the Buckley's. Cynthia, daughter-in-law of Sam Buckley, has clear memories of him and his work.

I knew the Cromford and High Peak Railway through visiting my grandmother who lived at Matlock Bath. My cousin and I used to crouch by a dry-stone wall, not far from the tunnel mouth, and watch the huge monsters that seemed to have fiery feet moving underneath their bodies. This was a thrill for both of us and it wasn't until many years later that my parents found out just how close we had been to the track.

Many years later when my boyfriend, Geoff Buckley, was about to go into the Royal Signals to do his National Service he took me home to meet his Dad who was an engine driver on the Cromford and High Peak Railway. Geoff and his three older brothers were close to their Dad, especially since their mother had died when Geoff was only fourteen. Geoff's father, Sam, with his smiling face and sparkling eyes, was typical of the engine drivers who had waved to me all those years before.

Geoff returned home in 1959 and we married in 1960. I spent many happy days in Wirksworth with Sam. I remember walking with him from Wirksworth to Middleton Top. Sam did that walk each and every day and, after a hard days work, must have been glad that the homeward walk was down-hill.

One wonderful summer's day we ran across the fields to where dad and Dennis Vallance, his fireman, had stopped the engine. The train was hauling the daily wagonloads to Parsley Hay and we climbed onto the foot-plate and began to ascend the Hopton incline.

The noise of the engine was something I shall never forget. The firebox was blazing red and more coal was shovelled into its hungry mouth. The noise reached a crescendo and Dad threw over the regulator and the engine and wagons continued the ascent to Hopton Top.

Driver Sam Buckley

From Alan Rimmer Collection

We couldn't tell anyone outside the family about this adventure because we shouldn't have been on the foot-plate, but I'm grateful that we were because neither Geoff or I have ever forgotten the experience.

Dad related many tales of the railway from the fearsome winters to the biting cold winds, the snow clearing and, when snow had drifted and filled the cutting, breaking through with the engine and seeing the icicles hanging from the tunnel roofs. Anyone who has walked along what is now the High Peak Trail in winter will know what I mean about the searing cold.

Dad and Dennis used to have boards put on the sides of the engine for a little protection. However Dad's weathered face, surrounding the bright eyes and beautiful smile, told of years of exposure to the elements.

Dad loved the countryside that he steamed through every day and the animals and birds that lived in it. The first skylark I ever heard was at Harborough Rocks and was pointed out to me by Dad. But there's another side to the countryside. The local hunt used to chase the hares over the fields and on more than one occasion dad had heard a hare screaming with an almost human voice. He used to love to be able to separate the huntsmen and hounds to give the terrified animal a fighting chance for life.

There were more sad times when myxomatosis plagued the rabbit population. The poor creatures wandered around with swollen heads and blind eyes. They had to be put out of their misery with a swift blow from a fireman's shovel. The carcasses were destroyed in the fire to try to stop the disease spreading. I remember Dad wondering how anyone could have deliberately caused the killer disease to be introduced to this country.

Dad told us stories of the railways, not all of them happy. An accident in October 1937 resulted in the engine and wagons being derailed and falling down over the embankment at the bottom of Hopton Incline. Geoff's father was working on the train and to begin with no one knew which man was seriously injured. Geoff's grandfather went to be with Geoff's mother. It turned out that tragedy was for another family, relief for ours. Geoff was born nine months later in July 1938.

When news of the closure of the line became a reality, Geoff took a holiday from work and photographed the engine and wagons, Dad and other members of staff at special vantage points along its journey at Newhaven Crossing, Gotham Curve and Harborough Rocks. Dad was only three months short of fifty years service when the line closed. He was sad about that.

The last train ran on a Sunday, a special for the Stephenson Locomotive Society. Dad wasn't driving it but was standing half-way up the hill with me. We couldn't know it at that moment but Sam was to become the very last driver on the Cromford and High Peak Railway.

Edward, Dad's second eldest son who at one time was Walter Spencer's fireman, was watching the ascent of Hopton incline with his son Ian and Geoff was taking photographs. As the engine came towards us Dad told me that they wouldn't make it to the top. I watched and sure enough the engine and wagon-loads of people had to roll back down the incline. A few wagons of people were detached and the train started off again, only to repeat the procedure. Then someone saw Dad and asked him to take the train up, so Dad and Edward, in their best suits, took the leading J94 and their load of railway enthusiasts over the summit for the last time. Lovely, but a very, very sad feeling for Dad and his family.

For several years, up until Geoff's Dad died in 1972, we went on holiday with my parents and Geoff's Dad to Austria. After arriving in France we always made a detour to visit the grave of my grandfather, Sergeant Edgar Woodcock of the 1/5th Sherwood Foresters who'd been killed in the First World War and is buried near Lapugnoy near Bethune. Dad was very touched to see all the cemeteries cared for by the Commonwealth War Graves Commission and by the fact that some of the headstones were made from the rough Hopton stone that he had transported years before on the Cromford and High Peak railway.

Some people scoff at railways, particularly the memories we have of steam trains, but perhaps they have not had the privilege that we have had. The many private lines that have been preserved throughout the country and maintained by volunteers are monuments in themselves to a lifestyle that has gone before. How fortunate I am to have known and loved such a great railwayman who was part of that heritage.

Cynthia Buckley

Amongst other long-service workers was William Morrin Handley whose daughter, Susan, recalls her early life.

My father, William Morrin Handley, was presented with a certificate for long service by the London Midland Region when he retired in 1978 but his railway career had begun on the Cromford and High Peak Line. First he was a plate-layer then a ganger. Eventually he made sub-inspector.

Dad's family lived at Brassington and he and my mother met when she took a teaching post at Brassington school. When they married they stayed in the village. This was early in the war but Dad was in a reserved occupation so he was in the Home Guard as well as doing his job.

I don't have many memories of living at Brassington because we moved to Hindlow when I was two-and-a-half but I used to go back to visit grandma and I loved it there. Grandma kept a pig in a stone building just across from their house. A cured ham would hang in their larder and we'd go and slice pieces off to fry for our breakfast. It was beautiful. I can still taste it.

I'd fetch the milk for Grandma from the farm down the hill. I had a small can, metal with a round handle, and the farmer's wife ladled the milk out of the big churns into it. Sometimes it was still warm from the cow.

It was a very safe place to be. Most people stayed and married people who came from their own area so everyone knew everybody else. Dad, taking his family out of the village, was an exception. Most of the mothers didn't work outside the home so they were there all day and everyone looked out for each other's children.

It was the same at Hindlow station near Breirlow Bar. There was a quarry office and a drying field where there was a washing line for us all to use, although I can never remember seeing it full of washing. The smuts from the railway and the dust from the quarry would have made it dirty as soon as it was hung out. Next to that was a terrace of six houses, a bungalow, a field and another terrace of six. The first house in the road was designated for the station-master but because he'd already got a house somewhere else it was rented out and that's where we lived. It was a bit posh because it was the only one that was double fronted and the only one to have a phone. The phone was really only meant to be used for railway business. If we wanted a line out we had to dial 201 and an operator would answer from a plug-in switchboard. We'd tell her the number we wanted and she'd connect us. When I was quite small I waited till my mum was upstairs and then phoned 201. I started chatting away about my doll's pram and dolls. I was thoroughly enjoying it until my mum came downstairs and caught me. I got a good slap for that!

Living at Hindlow was marvellous for children. We had plenty of freedom. There weren't any shops but we weren't bothered. The fishmonger and the butcher came round but the best was the ironmonger. He sold everything you could think of except food. It smelt wonderful, soap, paraffin, donkey stones to do the steps. Everything.

When the siren went to warn us the quarry was going to blast the whole community would rush outside, run across the road and up the hill. From the top of the hill we could see the rock falls. I was never hit by any but a piece went through the roof of number 6.

I used to get around quite a lot because mum used to take me with her when she was teaching. Before I started school properly mum was teaching at Taddington and we had to go from Hindlow to Buxton on the bus and change to another to get us out to Taddington. It meant leaving about six o'clock to get there by eight. I'd be sent to sit in the corner with a pile of books to keep me amused.

When she began teaching at Hardwick Square School in Buxton she took me along a couple of times before I joined the school. In all my years there I was never in her class. I think they did that deliberately.

I was an only child but I wasn't lonely. There were lots of children about and I had a dog, Punch, a wire-haired Fox Terrier. There was only six months between us. Punch's tail had been docked as a puppy and I learned to walk by holding onto his stub of a tail as we went round and round the table. I was fourteen when we had to have him put down and I walked and walked in the pouring rain, sobbing my heart out. I'd got a lot of memories of him though. With Dad working on the railway we had sleepers in the garden that were chopped up to burn on our range. They took some cutting and there were no electric saws then. Dad had made a shelter, a roof and sides, to keep them dry. Punch and I used to climb up on top of them and share Punch's dog biscuits. The only ones I didn't like were the black ones, charcoal I think they were. Punch got all of those.

Every year we went back to Brassington for Wakes Week. We had our own carnival and my dad, who was in the brass band, played the cornet. When I saw him dressed in his uniform with his chest puffed out like a turkey I was just so proud of him. We'd all march round the village and into the school playground where everything happened.

There was a fancy dress parade and one year I went as Joseph in his coloured coat. My mother had been crocheting a bed-spread in all different colours. It wasn't finished but I used it for my cloak and had a tea-towel tied round my head. There was a girl who dressed up as Bo-Peep and had a real lamb with her. She went into all sorts of carnivals and always won first prize so I thought I'd done very well to get second.

Dad's job meant we had free train passes; London, Brighton, Isle of Wight – we visited them all. We were lucky because most people weren't able to go on holiday because of the cost. Sometimes we'd have a trip to London and travel home in the warm train only to freeze when we changed trains for the last part of the journey. The trains were fast but the buses were the opposite. If we were going to Grandma's we got the train to Ashbourne then a bus to Brassington. Websters buses, based at Ashbourne, were very old and slow. It was all quite an adventure.

Dad sometimes worked nights because he couldn't work on the tracks when the trains were running. That meant I had him around during the days and sometimes we'd go for a walk. Dad would have his gun with him and suddenly he'd spot a rabbit for the pot and take aim. I never did like rabbit, perhaps because I'd seen them killed and watched my mother skinning them.

I was only four years old in the bad winter of 1947 but I can remember quite a lot about it. The snow must have been blowing from Buxton direction because the front of the houses, right to the top, were covered by the snow-drift and it reached out into the middle of the road. We could get out of the back door easily but for some reason dad began digging a tunnel out into the road. You'd have thought he'd had enough snow clearing with the railway. I don't know why he did it. Just a bit of fun I suppose.

I know the Hindlow tunnel was blocked with snow from four to nine feet high. They even used jet engines to blow the snow away but

Jet engines used as snow-blowers

digging out seemed the only thing that worked. They carted the snow away on a goods train.

Dad's railway career had begun on the Cromford and High Peak line as a plate-layer and then ganger. Later he became sub-inspector on the London and Midland Railway. He wasn't a big man, no more than five foot three, but they all called him 'Little Hitler'. He had a presence about him. When he finished he'd completed forty-two years on the railways.

I was just so proud of him.

Susan Howard

The High Peak area of Derbyshire is famous for its extremes of weather and just as Susan remembers the terrible winter of 1947 so too does Hubert Doxey.

The snow came down for several days and the whole line was at a standstill. Any men that were available, myself amongst them, were sent to snow-cut at Middleton Top. We began cutting at the Engine House and, supported by the shunt engines, reached 'Intake' crossing by nightfall.

The most productive way of working was to cut a grip of snow about eight to ten yards long then use the engine to burst into the snow ahead of the grip. That saved us several yards of cutting. Not that it was as easy as it sounds. Often the engine would get stuck in a large drift and we'd have to dig it out. Despite that it was still the quickest way of working.

As we walked home that night we though we had made a good start. We had but when we went back the following morning the snow that had still been falling, whipped up by a gale force wind, meant we were back to square one. That went on for five days, digging it out only to find it full again in the morning.

Eventually the main roads in the district were now cleared and traffic was able to run again. Many prisoners-of-war were still living in England and now they were able to get through on the road we were given fifty or sixty Germans to help with our work and a hundred or so Italian prisoners-of-war were helping to dig towards us from Parsley Hay.

When the German prisoners turned up it caused a lot of discontent. We had recently de-mobbed servicemen in our gang and one of them, Ron Goodall, was a former prisoner of war.

When we had our lunch-time sandwiches the only place we had to sit and eat them was the guard's van. We even had to take that in turns because the van was so small. The Germans had their lunches in the British Restaurant in Wirksworth where they were treated to a hot meal. That didn't please us, either.

Our boss, Mr Merrill, had an intense dislike of the German prisoners-of-war, a dislike that they felt just as strongly towards him. One day the prisoners dug under a large drift. Merril shouted to Arthur Millward 'Go and see what they want.' Off went Arthur and he disappeared. We all rushed over and dug him out and Merril went over to the Germans and assured them he was too old a cat to be caught by a bunch of kittens.

After many days snow-cutting we arrived at Longlciffe on a Sunday afternoon. Brassington and the small surrounding settlements had not had supplies of coal or food for days apart from any that was dropped from aircraft. Jack Smith said 'First thing in the morning we'll bring coal and water for the people of Brassington.'

When we went to work on Monday another great fall of snow, helped by high winds, had again blocked the line and once more we started cutting from the engine house. It was several days before we again reached Longcliffe and Jack Smith, once bitten, twice shy, sent the train crew back for the coal and water.

Harold Wain and I went on cutting at Longcliffe and after quite a

Prisoners of War employed in snow clearance

time Harold said 'Look, someone's left a pipe in. That could have been dangerous.'
I poked my shovel down alongside the pipe and hit something. 'Listen,' I said, 'that's the rail. I'd have thought it would have been deeper.'
We dug away at the snow only to find the pipe was the chimney of the guards van and what I thought was the rail was the metal runners on the van. The snow we'd been cutting was on top of the van.

When we left Longcliffe there were plenty more cuttings that were full of snow and the only place we could put the snow was over the top of the cutting. We had to carry it all by hand because the engines were useless in those conditions. The drifts were up to twenty feet deep so we had to remove it in four lifts. It took ages because it took four men to remove one shovel full of snow. Three ledges were cut into the snow, each one around four feet higher than the one below, with a man on each ledge. The snow was then thrown up ledge to ledge and finally over the top of the cutting.

One particular day it was so cold that Jack Smith collapsed and only recovered when we got him to the guard's van to warm him up.

Some weeks after the start of the snow blizzards the thaw set in and the great drifts began to sink. As the snow levels went down we found rabbits still frozen to telegraph wires.

Hubert Doxey

For some people the railways offered an opportunity for a change of direction.

'You're better than that and you've got to do something better.' That's what my dad, who worked in the quarries, said. There was the emphasis, especially in our family, that you had to do better than your father. You were expected to do it.

Any railway worker needed to be skilled but the Cromford and High Peak Line needed skills that were that little bit different.

We learned our jobs just by being there. It was a case of watching somebody else do it and then, when he thought you were ready, he'd say, 'Well, it's time you had a go.' We had a long apprenticeship, building up experience in various circumstances until we become competent.

Every engine was different. The accident in 1937 was all about a particular engine approaching Hopton Incline in a particular way because that was the only way that engine could manage to get up it. If we wanted to take an engine up Hopton Incline we'd set off from Middleton Top and by the time we'd entered the Intake Tunnel we'd have already built a good head of steam. We'd make sure we'd got water in the boiler, half a glass of water to drive it, and we'd notch it up on our gears almost to half way. Once we were at the bottom of the bank we could start letting extra steam into the cylinders, giving us that extra bit of power.

Later on they brought in engines that had an entirely different way of working. With the old 'North Londons' you wanted speed to get up the inclines. Later the J94's were brought in and they had a much stronger engine. You could depend on that strength to pull you up. As long as you didn't prime it! That's lifting water out of the boiler with the steam into the cylinders. Steam in cylinders is all right but water is an incompressible material and if it becomes trapped between the cylinder cover and piston it causes mayhem. Steam expands. Water doesn't. If the very worst happens the cylinder head blows off.

We knew exactly what to do and when to do it. On one trip we were about half-way to the tunnel and the fireman put the injectors on. I knocked them off straight away. I mean you don't climb Hopton Bank with injectors on.

I've been on the footplate when Dad started off at the bottom of Hopton Incline. We went faster and faster and the engine reached a

Sheep Pasture 1953. Left to right: Sam Hall, Inspector Jack Smith and Herbert Hallows

© Derbyshire Advertiser/Alan Rimmer Collection

crescendo of noise then he threw over the regulator and it carried on up. Just for that one split second it sounded as if all hell had broken loose then the regulator worked and she just went up. To get it right was a fantastic feeling!

'L.M.S! Little May Smith - that's what everyone called me.'

'Everyone' was right. Little May, now in her eighties, is under five feet tall and as slim as she was as a girl. It didn't stop her from taking on not just one job that was traditionally seen as being men's work, but several.

I was only sixteen and still at school when I met my husband, Jack. I was visiting a girlfriend at Hurdlow and I hopped off the train and there Jack stood, waiting to take my ticket. And that's where it all started from. If he was on the right shift he'd be waiting for me outside the school and give me a lift on his motor-bike.

Not long after that I left school and went to work as a secretary to the manager of Friden Brickworks. To get to work I caught the train to Hartington and then walked it to Friden. If a lorry came along, going to the works to be loaded, I'd thumb a lift.

We knocked-off work at five o'clock and had to walk the two or three miles, in the dark in winter, from Friden to Hartington to catch the train home.

When I wasn't working for the manager I was doing a job that was really meant for men. When the wagons came through to go up to the quarry I took their numbers and when they came back down loaded I used the pulley weighing machine to weigh them out and invoice them. I loved the work but sometimes the workers weren't that easy to get along with. There were women working in the brick works. Women are more catty than men and they used to take the mickey a bit out of the office staff. A bit of jealousy I think. I was really timid and when the women came down in their rough aprons – it was a dusty job – I was frightened to death of them. I was always pleased when the works manager took me to work in his little office in the yard, well away from the women.

When Jack and I were getting married I gave my notice in because in those days married women stayed home and took care of the house and family. We had to live at Friden because Jack was working there and the house went with the job. We were there eighteen months, living in one of the two railway houses, and it was terribly grim. We even had to go to Parsley Hay to get our water that was brought up in a tanker. The Rangers use the houses now as store rooms.

I always knew we would move around quite a lot because Jack was ambitious. He went to signalling classes then he carried on studying because he didn't intend staying all his working life as a signal-man.

Once the war started I had to look for work again because everyone had to work outside the home. If we didn't find our own jobs then one would be found for us. I knew the foreman at Beswick's Limeworks at Hindlow and he put a word in for me and I got a job in the works office. I did the clock cards and if the workers were a minute late they had a quarter of an hour knocked off. I used to hate doing that especially as they came from a long way away, as far afield as Butterton, Grindon, Cauldon Low. Some came on motorbikes, others came part way with somebody and hitched a lift for the rest of the way.

After the war I took on the job of Porter. It was unusual for a woman to do that work but that's what I did, excepting that Jack and I sorted it out between us. I was supposed to meet the train from Parsley Hay and take the wagon numbers and all the particulars but Jack used to do that bit of the job and I did the office work.

It was a good time. We were very proud to have our own Morgan three-wheeler. Both Jack and I enjoyed dancing and having the car meant we could go dancing at Hartington and the Pavilion Gardens in Buxton. When we did the Lancers Jack would lift me up and swing me round. Once we'd got our daughter, Glenys, we realised we needed a bigger house. At that time Jack was at Middleton Top and there were no houses in Wirksworth for strangers like us. Anyway Jack managed to get the Crossing House but there was a problem. The house had the crossing-keeper's job that went with it, a job I'd have to do.

'Oh, no,' I said, because I'd only just come out of hospital with Glenys but Jack said it wasn't a big job and he could help me in the mornings. Of course, I ended up saying 'yes' and that's how we got the house and how I came to do that job for over thirty years!

The crossing had four gates, a signal-box and a distance signal right down the track – 'they called it Forty Steps' - so I worked as the signal-box woman as well. I had to be there to work the gates so I'd run across the road, up the signal-box steps, flick some levers across to release the points in the road that were holding the gates, twist the wheel round, then lock the gates with the same lever and put the signals right.

To begin with there weren't too many trains. The first one in the morning was about half-past six and either Jack would run across or I would, it didn't matter. The last one was about five o'clock. But then we began to get all this railway traffic through from Wirksworth, carrying the sugar beet. The limestone from the top end of Wirksworth and Middleton is very pure and when they crushed and pulped the beet they used it as a filter to get rid of the impurities. It was that purified sugar that went into the Tate and Lyle packets. It was harvested in September and October and I was letting trains through at half-past-seven and nine o'clock at night. There weren't many sidings at High Peak Junction and Cromford Goods so there wasn't that much room for the wagons. If they were very behind with the sugar beet they'd run Sundays too. When you're a resident crossing-keeper you're on call twenty-four hours a day.

I was sixty-two by the time they finished me and the railway had been closed. The trains and gates had gone. The old fence is still there – and the lights. The signal-box has gone to Rowsley South. I've not been down to the station recently but I've been told it's like a little forest. There's trees growing absolutely everywhere.

I really loved that house. They were happy days. Very happy.

May Smith

For another young woman who lived in Tissington the railways were to affect her whole future.

I was seventeen and living with my parents. My friend, Ivy, said 'Come on, Mary, let's go and have a look at the new porters, see what they're like.' And I can tell you there were more than us who went! I'd never had a boyfriend before. If I'd brought a lad home when I was younger I'd have been in trouble.

John had come to Tissington as a porter in 1937 to escape unemployment in Cumbria. He was always going to better himself and he only stayed at Tissington for a year before he got a better porter's job in Buxton. Promotion didn't come automatically, it was dead man's shoes all the time. You might have taken all the exams and passed them years before but until someone left or died there wouldn't be a job for you. That's why he had to take any chance that came his way. Some workers were in the same job for fifty years even though they were qualified to move up.

John and I courted for five years before we married in 1942 and moved to the railway cottages at Blackwell Mill at the bottom of the Pike where we stayed for seventeen years. There were three lines then, one towards Sheffield, one to Buxton and the main one that went to Miller's Dale. One day I was cooking lunch, took my eye of my son, George, for just one minute, turned around and he'd disappeared. A few minutes later the signal-man rang to tell me George was on the line and was crying. Oh, that was a time. It was probably all over in minutes but it felt as if it had gone on forever.

Tissington Station

One night when John was going along Ashwood Dale he noticed a piece of loose line and reported it. The railway company paid him a one pound reward because it could have caused a nasty accident. That was a lot of money in those days.

John worked for the railway for forty years and died in service in 1977.

Mary Maxwell

The trains carried many different materials, from limestone to cheeses to pigeons.

There wasn't a train went by on the Buxton to Ashbourne line that didn't have pigeons on it. There were no end of pigeon racers and you could guarantee that by the time you got to Ashbourne you'd have forty or fifty baskets of racing pigeons. They'd train them up for the big races by letting them go at Ashbourne and they'd all fly home.

Every station had its characters, people that have been remembered through the anecdotes that have been handed down through generations. Hartington was no exception.

Frank Waring, a shunter at Friden, had always worked in the quarries and he had a fancy way of lacing his boots. He'd tie a knot in his lace, put it in the first lace hole, then he'd wrap it round his boot and tuck it in. Someone said to him 'My word Frank, that's a rum way to tie your laces'.

Frank said 'But I always lace me boots like that. I've worked in quarries and if you gets your foot trapped you've only got to nick the lace and you can pull it straight out. No buggering about getting laces out.'

'Just get me one of them engine brushes. They're just the job for brushing beasts down before we do milking'. Frank Waring.

Nearly all the cheese made in the factory at Hartington used to go by rail and George Gibbs used to bring them up to the station. Now George had a nick-name – 'Mr. Suki'. Goodness knows why. There were two porters at Hartington Station, Arthur Foost and Charlie Eley. When my dad first went there these two other workers kept on and on, 'Mr. Suki'll be up soon. Mr. Suki'll be up soon.'

My dad thought that was his name so when he arrived my dad says 'Good evening Mr. Suki. I'm Arthur Robinson, the new station master.' And Suki says 'You're a cheeky bugger, Arthur.'

One of the earliest uses of the old High Peak Railway was transporting iron ore to Friden Wharf. It was mined just above Wages Lane and taken to Friden by horse and cart. One of the carters in the 1840's was a local lad, John Holywell, who went on to become Premier of British Columbia.

Friden Brickworks and High Peak Silica had opened up once there was a railway to transport their goods. They depended on it completely.

Magnesium was produced in 'crowns' and nine crowns went into a forty gallon drum. It was intended that the magnesium would be sent via Matlock up to Buxton and on to Manchester. That's where the railway fell down the first time. The firm wanted a daily delivery and the railway bosses said there was no way they could provide a daily service.

In some ways the sales promotion of the railways was very bad. They weren't really interested in small freight, daily freight. Because of this the material was brought down spasmodically.

More revenue came from the transporting of a compound called ferrosilica or iron silicate which is a hard, black material that was used in the process of producing magnesium. It came by ship to Hull, then continued the journey by rail on the Hull and Barnsley Railway. They had to use special wagons to get them down the High Peak Line that were brought through Buxton and Friden and then lowered down the Hopton incline by a locomotive and shunted back down to the siding.

The building of the magnesium plant resulted in the modernisation of the Sheep Pasture incline. Both Middleton Top and Sheep Pasture engines were looked at but it was decided that the Middleton engine could cope with the increased traffic. So they set to and designed a new electric winding winch that was installed in Sheep Pasture engine room. By the time it was built and installed the traffic had virtually disappeared and that's typical of the way the railways worked.

The magnesium factory failed for two reasons. One was the fact that the Japanese could actually make it cheaper than us; at the time our price was £110 a ton and they could do it for £90. Secondly the plant was built in the wrong place. Local dolomite limestone was used in the production of magnesium. The plant should have been built on the Western side where it is 100% dolomite because the East side is riddled with clay veins that ultimately affected the purity of the magnesium. There'd have been no problems and it could have still been running today.

It helped to have a sense of humour when working the railways.

'Right, you've got so many coaches on for Parsley Hay,' the guard said to the driver. Now normally the driver would pull away from the platform slowly so that a guard could get into his guard's van as it was going past, but this time, as soon as the guard told the driver how many he had on, the driver went like the clappers. He was going so fast that the guard didn't have a hope of getting on. He'd set off running after us and the driver slowed down until the guard thought he could get in his van and then the driver'd set off again. It was done just for devilment!

There was a sharp turn going into Hartington Station quarry. To get the empties right down into the quarry they used to 'hit them up'.

They'd step back a bit and the empties, eight or nine, would go on their own. Cooper, one of the quarry men, would be down the quarry and they'd drop the brakes and stop the wagons where they were needed. 'Spotty' Robinson had a Wessy engine and he hit it up and overdid it a bit. He slammed the brake on and of course he goes past the 'stop' board, the board that said 'LMS engines STOP', because the curve was too sharp for locos. He went about an engine's length beyond the 'stop' board and 'Bang' - he was off the rails and on the floor.

'Oh, bloody hell,' he said. 'I'll get the sack. I went by a 'stop' board about a month ago and they gave me a warning then. I'll get the sack.'

They'd sent for the breakdown gang to get the engine back on again so, while they waited for them to come, the porter, the fireman and my dad dug the 'stop' board up. Further up the track they dug another hole and put the stop board in that. When the breakdown comes, and after they'd got the engine on, the fellow in charge says 'That board's no good there, it wants to be back here.'

Anyway everything was squared up and away they went. After they'd all gone they dug the board up again, moved it back to where it had been and put it in. A few days later three men came from Stoke. They dug up the board, measured back twenty yards or so, dug another hole and put it in. When they'd gone Dad and the others dug it up again and put it back in the same hole again. And he got away with it, did Spotty Robinson!

Ron Riley

There were occasions when the humour was directed at people who had no idea they were the butt of a joke.

When the fox hunt was going through we'd often stop the train. Some of the riders used to get into the railway and couldn't get out. My old mate used to say 'Edward, stop the train. Go on and open that gate.'

We'd let them through saying 'Thank you very much Sir,' knowing we'd given the fox a bit of a chance to get away.

However happy people were to work for the railways there was another side that all too many people saw when faced with difficulties. Anyone unfortunate enough to be injured would be left without the means to earn a living, without the money to take care of their families and retirement pensions hadn't been invented.

There was no real retirement age, they just kept people on as long as they were fit and able. They'd be hard pressed to manage if they finished work. What were they meant to live on?

Billy, from way back, lost a leg and when he came back to work he helped out in the workshops. They kept him on a good ten years after retirement age. He wasn't alone. A lot of people worked fifty years.

Improved conditions of service were needed but the employers made sure they didn't lose too much money when their workers were injured.

There was a Workman's Compensation Act but there was no benefit until the person was back at work. All the weeks in hospital they got nothing. They weren't going to pay anything out until they knew those that were ill would be returning to work.

When the 1937 accident happened they thought Bill Bowden wasn't badly hurt and sent him off to the Cottage Hospital in Wirksworth. All they could see of my dad was his arm sticking out of the coal and they rushed him to Derby thinking there was no hope for him. Father, along with three other workers, survived and Bill Bowden died

I was nearly ten and I only got to hear about it when I got home from school. I can remember it very clearly because it was the day I

Accident at the foot of Hopton Incline, 6th October 1937
in which Driver W Boden was fatally injured

was due to join the church choir and the family thought I'd be better off carrying on as normal. 'You get along,' they said and that was it.

I didn't realise how bad he was because nobody said much about it but there was gloom and despondency around the house.

Of course with no insurance in those days the hospital bills took all of their savings. We struggled for a while but if we hadn't had any savings I don't know what we'd have done.

Geoff Kirk

Later on railway workers had two-pence a week stopped out of their pay and that gave them free access to Wirksworth Cottage Hospital and Derby Royal Infirmary. But the local doctor still had to be paid.

There was a man whose wife was ill and he ran all the way from Middleton to the Doctor's House. He rang the bell and the Doctor leaned through an upstairs window and asked what was the matter. The man told him and the Doctor asked 'Can you pay?'

It's such a short time ago. It all changed with the National Health Service in 1948 but before that it was a part of life. People didn't get any help from the family either, or not more than a little, because they had so little themselves. It was just a case of tightening belts and pulling together.

The strange thing is that if you look back to the mid-eighteen-hundreds things were better than in the nineteen hundreds. In 1844 a bloke got killed on the Midland Railway and in January 1845 the Directors awarded him a pension of £250 at 4% interest a year. This was put in trust for the family. So if they were doing that in those days it would have seemed natural that the railway companies wouldn't want to be seen as refusing to look after their workers.

July 1955 – Upended by accident into the Station House garden at Steeplehouse

Alan Rimmer Collection

Railway families that had suffered injury or bereavement did have some help offered to them. The children of the family could be cared for in the Railway Orphanage in Derby. For the children who received this help life became bewildering as they struggled with harsh discipline, no affection and the thought of many years of care ahead of them before they would be back with their families.

The O'Shaughnessy Family

I suppose we all think our families and the lives of those in it are just ordinary, the same as so many other people, but it's not true. Every family has a different story to tell, one that is individual to them. My story is about a family who had someone working on the railways from the early part of the last century, first of all with the Midland Railway and then the Cromford and High Peak.

I'll take you back to the beginning. Mathew, my father, was born in 1891 in Normanton, West Yorkshire. When he was about sixteen years old the family moved a mile or two from the house he'd been born in to the end house on Station Road. That same year a family moved into West View which was back-to-back with Station Road and had a narrow, cobbled lane that separated the two rows of houses. Little did my father know that eleven year old Alice Woodcock, the eldest child of that family, would become his wife.

Mathew and Alice married on 10th April, 1918 at St. John's Roman Catholic Church in Normanton. Mathew was twenty-seven and a boilermaker's labourer working for the Midland line. Alice, at twenty-one, worked as a munitions worker and both their fathers were miners. The newly-weds remained in the town and by the end of the General Strike in 1926 Mathew and Alice were a well-established couple with five children. But things were about to change.

The General Strike had been a difficult time for ordinary people.

Many railway-workers suffered economic deprivation when, amongst other industries, railway services were suspended and many workers were made redundant. Mathew was 'asked' to move from Normanton to work on the Cromford and High Peak Railway and a few months later his family joined him. They managed to rent a local authority house that was fairy new, well built and had a reasonably large garden for their five children. It wasn't long before they moved again, going only a matter of a hundred yards further up the hill. This was an older property with more bedrooms, and, according to Alice, there was less rent to pay.

All the O'Shaughnessy children went to North Street School and, because they were Roman Catholics, attended the little church at Gorsey Bank for Mass every Sunday morning and catechism in the afternoons.

The final addition to their family arrived on 16th October 1933 when Eileen was born at Wirksworth Cottage Hospital. Sadly she was destined to have no recollections of our father because May 1935 brought disaster to the family. Mathew had been ill earlier in the year and had never really recovered. On the 23rd May he died from the effects of rheumatic fever, meningitis and pneumonia. My father was taken back to his roots and was buried in his birthplace, Normanton.

He was only forty-three when he died and I was coming up to nine so my memories of him are those of a young boy. I remember a dad who was firm but never oppressively so; a dad who carried me on the crossbar of his bike; a dad who came to school to collect me and carried me up Cromford Hill when the snow was too deep for a little 'un.

We used to visit him occasionally at Sheep Pasture Top and sit in the small cabin with the men whilst they had their lunch break. We toasted our bare knees that were only inches from the banked-up coal fire. One memorable occasion we had a ride down to the bottom of the incline and back in one of the wagons but I had to walk back after a ride to Steeple Grange on the footplate. We'd go to look at the winding house, particularly the big wheel with the cable round it, and the noises, the smells and the feeling of power made it into a treat.

When my father died my mother was left bereft and in dire financial straits. She had six children to care for although the eldest one, Walter, who was just sixteen was working full time as an engine cleaner on the LMS at Derby. It was clear that mother had to do something to help the family. The solution was not a happy one. Mother decided that my brother and I should go into the Railway Servants' Orphanage on Ashbourne Road in Derby. In August 1935, just three months after our father had died, we were taken to the orphanage.

The beginnings of the orphanage were rooted in the fact that the railways not only brought employment and financial security but also injury and death to some of its workers. It soon became clear there was a need to provide care for the children of railway workers and the orphanage was supported by money donated by railwaymen who gave two shillings a year to the fund. What had started in 1875 for eleven children was providing a home for twenty by the end of the first year and a Matron was employed to care for the children whose numbers continued to rise year by year.

What had begun as a means of providing care for children swiftly became a place where children were known by numbers rather than names, where they were not allowed to talk at meal times and where brothers and sisters were separated. The regime was harsh. We were allowed a visit from home on one afternoon a month and during the long summer holidays we could go home if our families were able to have us. We were lucky because our family lived in the area but other children who lived hundreds of miles away never got to see their families.

This was a far from happy time. We had not only lost our father but the rest of the family too. We'd gone from living with our brothers and sisters to sharing with many other children who we did not know. It must have been a very sad time for our mother too, who was still grieving for our father when she had to send us away.

Within a very short time my mother realised that a move to Derby would be in the family's interest. My mother found lodgings at Douglas Street in Derby. That was in 1936. For my brother and I this was a good move. Not only could we go home during the long summer holidays but we were also allowed to visit one Saturday afternoon a month. That was until the outbreak of war when the children at the orphanage were evacuated to Fritchley and my brother and I were back to visiting during the summer holidays.

Years later a Home Office inspection revealed the harsh treatment meted out to the children and the orphanage was threatened with closure 'unless drastic action is taken to improve the lifestyle and environment of the children'. In 1948 the 'drastic action' came in the form of Miss Marjorie Seaver, the new Lady Superintendent for the orphanage. It was too late for us but future children were to benefit from her change of regime. Within a few weeks of Miss Seaver taking up her appointment the children were being called by their names, the rigid systems used in the orphanage were changed and the children began to be given affection and encouragement. The home was re-named St. Christopher's, and that is what it remained until its closure in 1990.

My brother Walter was the only son to carry on the railway tradition. He worked his way up from cleaner to his call-up to the Armed Forces, then fireman to driver. He was a keen union man and eventually became Secretary of the Derby branch of the NUR. Walter had no truck with the man in the street's nostalgia about the glories of steam. For him they were dirty and hard work and diesels were easier to handle. Perhaps if I'd worked the engines I'd have felt the same but I didn't. For me those 'Snorting Horses' hurtling out of the tunnels were marvellous. They were alive!

George O'Shaughnessy

North London Tank on the 1 in 4 gradient approaching top of Hopton incline

The 'dead-man's-shoes' method of promotion didn't take into consideration our capabilities. But taking it all round I think it was the fairest system you could get because there was no favouritism with it. If anybody was dissatisfied with it the only way he could do anything about it was to move. There was no right of appeal.

Many years ago I worked at Hatfield in a little locomotive depot on the northern fringes of London. There were men there who were still firemen when they were fifty-five years old. No vacancies had turned up and they didn't want to move away to get a drivers job and more money because they didn't want to uproot their families.

The working conditions would probably never have changed without the Unions. Inevitably there were tensions between union members and those who wouldn't join.

One man carried on working whilst there was a strike going on and his life was made an absolute misery. He was so isolated. The strikers turned up day after day to intimidate him as he went through the gate and a group of them would stand all day long waiting for him to come out. In fact there was very little work for him to do because there were no trains getting through to the line.

The tension caused no end of trouble in families and between those whose jobs placed them in other Railway Unions. Around our table at home we had a driver and a fireman who were in ASLEF, a signalman in the NUR and two clerks in the TSSA . I'm not saying there were rows but there could be a great deal of friction on different issues.

At the time of the '55 strike I can remember my dad saying 'You'd better come to live with us lad. It's going to be hard.'

Over the years things did change but not always for the better.

In the 1960's, age discrimination began to come into it. Before that it was experience that counted. They started taking more account of graduates with paper qualifications that took precedence over years of experience.

Years earlier I'd had a similar experience. I was working in the drawing office and applied for a job in research. The man in charge of the department was going to interview me and wanted to know my qualifications.

'I've got a Higher National Certificate with endorsements in Mechanical Engineering,' I told him.

'Oh dear,' he said. 'That's unfortunate. Within this department we prefer that our staff are all graduates. We want everyone to have a degree.' It didn't matter what degree they'd got. Anything would do – even if it was Biology. Or so he said.

People who'd taken Higher National Certificates and Diplomas had completed them at the same time as undertaking an apprenticeship. If the firm was generous the worker was paid for his one day a week at Technical College but this was counterbalanced by the fact that the worker would have to study at least one and often two evenings a week as well. That way I ended up with both a paper qualification and experience. I did get the job within the research department and I stayed until I retired but I felt like one of the 'also ran's' because of the other peoples' attitudes.

Alan Rimmer

But the winds of change were blowing in a way that would effect villagers, people who lived in local small towns and, particularly, the men who worked on the railways.

May Smith

Cynthia Buckley

Susan Howard

George O'Shaughnessy

Hubert Doxey, MBE

Derrick Wain

Alan Rimmer

Andy Pollock

Rick Jillings

Steve Farren

Ron Riley

Bill Hallows

Driver Sam Buckley and Sam Radford exchanging train staffs at Longcliffe, 21st April, 1967

The last service train from Parsley Hay to Middleton Top descending Hopton Incline 21st April, 1967

© Derbyshire Advertiser/Alan Rimmer Collection

A TIME OF CHANGE

In 1967 Prime Minister Harold Wilson grappled with the devalued pound, newspapers reported the death of the great actor Spencer Tracy and the people of the High Peak saw the end of their railways. Tracks were ripped up to be replaced by grasses, sleepers found their way to numerous gardens and children began to use the old railway line as a perfect place for playing.

I was born at Cromford so it was just part of my life that when I woke up in the morning and looked out of the back door I'd see them stoking up the chimney at Sheep Pasture. I could see the engine coming along the top and I knew that the school bus would get to the top of the hill while the engine was taking water at Black Rocks. They were things I thought would last forever. I couldn't imagine them not being there.

The writing was on the wall. It was inevitable. You can't run a company at a loss and that's what was happening. At one point the only work for the railway was to carry water to Parsley Hay, where there wasn't any running water. In the last few years it ran to bring the coal and water to the engine house so that the railwaymen could actually run the line by bringing the coal and water etc. etc.

There's a lot said about Beeching but all he did was highlight what was happening. The High Peak was nothing to do with him. The closure came out of the thinking of the day that everything had to pay without cross-subsidisation.

Many of the railway workers had left before the closure, others found new jobs and some were made redundant.

The timing of the closure worked well for the men who were being made redundant. Until the National Agreement that had been drawn up during the Wilson government around 1964-65 they'd have got nothing. Most of them were near retirement age and didn't have long to wait for their pensions so they were all right financially.

Some of them took redundancy payouts and started back for the same firm a week later in a different department. I know a few who are still working as consultants for private firms even now. One said he'd been asked to go back for a day and the last time I spoke to him he was getting a bit fed up because he was working as many hours as he had before.

Anyone who was transferred to another depot received travelling expenses until they were promoted. One driver got them until he retired.

Things moved quickly once the railways had stopped running.

Ward's came in and cleared the lines up within a couple of months. The lines went for scrap metal but the sleepers were sold on and were in high demand. Tom Beeston had a paper to say he could buy some and so did Sam Buckley who went off with his three lads and carried them to where Issac's coal yard used to be. The idea was he'd get a lorry to pick them up and take them home. It wasn't to be. Old Tom went down to the yard and said 'Those'll be mine' and took them away. Sam Buckley was livid.

I didn't come out and take photographs of the track being lifted and so on. Probably because I didn't want to see it being dismantled.

What had been a bustling, if not thriving, industry had disappeared in a matter of months. Derbyshire County Council and the Peak National Park wanted to buy the railways to turn them into recreational trails. Negotiations began but it was to be another four years before Ken Harwood was appointed as the first Countryside Ranger and the transformation began.

The trails have a lot of atmosphere, particularly when we go through the tunnels.'

Maria and Ken
Harwood with Nelly

I came for the interview and whilst they were making up their minds I took a walk along Cromford Canal and up Sheep Pasture. And a very derelict site it was. Little bits of railway hardware lay about all over the place and everything looked dilapidated. There were motorbikes and airguns just thrown about and I thought 'Oh, blimey. Do I really want this?'

But I did. I knew I did. We'd had to think hard about me going for the job. Financially it was a big drop and we had two tiny children. We'd gone over and over it.

At that time we lived in Hayfield at the foot of Kinder Scout and I was working for a small private tool-making firm in New Mills. From my workplace I could look out of the window and see Kinder. I spent my weekends up there and I couldn't help thinking it would be better to spend five days up there and two down here. In summer I'd come home from work and instead of having tea I'd grab a packet of banana sandwiches and set off up the Scout with the kids. I always wanted to be outside. I loved the countryside.

I'd been a volunteer and a part-timer with the Peak Park Planning Board since 1954 and twice I'd applied for jobs but didn't get them. The change in the Countryside Act meant local councils could set up amenity sites and that's how the trails job began. A lot of National Park part-time Rangers got full time jobs around the country.

About eighteen of us went on the High Peak Trail and stopped at Parsley Hay for ice-creams. We all used the toilets before we moved off and two miles later realised we were one short. I'd counted everyone in and out once but one lady had gone back in again. Funnily enough her husband hadn't even noticed she was missing.

For Ken's wife, Maria, the change produced mixed feelings.

I was pleased that Ken had got the job he really wanted and had been working towards for years. Every other week-end he'd be out working on The Park, all without pay. He became an assistant Ranger and was in charge of a small group of part-timers. His life was wrapped up in it. He might have been a tool-maker by day but his love of the countryside was such that he wanted to learn more about it. So he went to Manchester University and did extra-mural courses on geology and botany. He was perfect for the job. On the other hand we were leaving friends behind and Ken's parents. And the house went with the job; we weren't given an option. We didn't know whether to sell our house or rent it out but eventually we decided to sell. It was just before the house-price boom but having bought it for three thousand we sold it for four-and-a-half so felt we'd made a good profit. When we moved into Middleton we put the money into the bank thinking it was our security blanket but the house we'd sold was worth thirty-thousand pounds within a year. We couldn't have bought it back if we'd wanted to.

We spent a lot of time considering the best way of managing our money. One thing we knew for certain was that if Ken left his job the County Council were under no obligation to re-house us. In spite of Ken's wages going down we knew we'd have to save regularly to make sure we'd got something behind us and that later on we could prove to a building society that we were capable of paying a mortgage. Eventually it paid dividends but it tied us to the house and to the site.'

Whilst the family got used to living on an old railway track in a house where generations of railway workers had grown up Ken started to develop his job.

It's very exciting starting something that is entirely new. The County didn't have much idea of how they wanted the trails to develop. They were new to the game and I had an almost clear field as to how I tackled it. I'd got my own ideas and it went the way I wanted it to in the early days.

There were two sides to the job; conservation work and the visiting public. I knew there had to be a compromise between the two and that the conservation work would make the trails more interesting for walkers, so there had to be a balance. In the early days I used to involve the local schools in tree planting schemes. We've always had a dog and I took her with me wherever I went. She wasn't part of the job but she

Cotesfield Farm and Bridge on the High Peak Trail

was a marvellous tool because children crowded round to make a fuss of her and they'd gell straight away. You're there. You've got them.

That was marvellous and had a really good effect on the outcome of the trails. At that time the Black Rock area was awful. It used to get ripped about, the kids didn't take much care of it. But once they'd planted trees they made sure they were never damaged. We'd find rings of stones round some of them and the children would put moss round the roots to protect them. They were watching what they had planted and it was a great success. That was in the mid-seventies and it's a good feeling that all these years on they might remember planting and looking after those trees. I'm happy when I look at those I planted and I hope those children, long since grown, are too.

Certainly Ken and Maria's children were happy and it is a time Maria remembers with affection.

It was a lovely place for the children, a wonderful place to grow up in, and they had a good childhood. They had friends who visited our house but if they wanted to go out it depended on whether I could take them because Ken wasn't often around. It could have been isolating but we knew we had to make a definite point of going out and making friends. It was the Ranger Service that gave us our social life and we're still friends with many of the people from that time in our lives.

Despite living at Middleton our children don't have the same feelings about the countryside as we do. We were both born in the outskirts of cities and we fully appreciated where we were and what we were doing. We've never lost that and it is still magic to us now. For our children the countryside was there every day. When our son had been to stay with his grandma in Sheffield in the same week that we'd all watched a family of owls, all he reported in his school news book was that he'd been on a bus!

Maria was not only married to Ken but also worked for him as a part-time Ranger.

Ken was a champion of the people and a good boss and fought hard for the things he believed in. At the beginning the Council wouldn't allow dogs on the trails because of sheep. Ken fought it and the Council backed down, agreeing dogs could be on the trails but must be on leads. Ken fought that too with the result that dogs could run free.

Whoever was working with him was always part of the team, no matter whether they were part-timers, volunteers, whatever. They were all dedicated people and Ken recognised that.

It was Ken's wish that, no matter what the time was, nobody left the site until the last Ranger was back off patrol. In those days we didn't have radios or mobile phones. There was no way of contacting people once they'd gone out. Even when radios were introduced we always waited for the last person to come in.

Ken can easily place where his approach came from.

A lot of my ideas and feelings were nurtured because I liked walking and joined a group that started 'Wardening'. The Head Ranger of the Peak District National Park was Tom Tomlinson. I loved his attitude to everything. He was so calm, never got roused no matter what was going on. He'd just go straight in and tackle it. And I thought 'This is the way' and I tried to emulate him as much as I could. He was a marvellous man.

I'd worked in Mountain Rescue on the gritstone of Crowden, Bleaklow and Kinder Scout but I didn't imagine rescuing would be part of my new job; I was mistaken. The police called us out on several occasions when people had gone missing. One evening we'd finished our duty, had our de-briefing and were settled in the Rising Sun having a pint. The landlord took a call from the police who wanted us to go

This is a perfect English day. The trails are beautiful and the views are wonderful. We feel really comfortable here.
Elderly man from south Derbyshire.

to East Crack on Black Rock where a climber had got his knee trapped. East Crack is nasty. It gets smaller as it goes down and is wider at the back than the front. We got roped-up, went down and couldn't shift him. He wasn't frightened – he wasn't going anywhere. Somebody had a bright idea and set off for the chip shop at Wirksworth. He brought back a load of fat and poured it down the crack. Out he came. You could smell chips on East Crack for ages.

Because the trails were walled either side I didn't think people could get lost; do you want to bet? How many nights were we out looking for folks who just didn't turn up? Plenty. If anyone had fallen down the embankment we'd never have seen them so the Landrover had special lights that shone down the sides. It came in useful when an elderly gentleman had hired a bike and didn't return. Fortunately the cycle-hire attendant remembered him and we began searching the trail. Then we called the police in and we were out all night looking for him. Eventually the police traced his home address where his wife told them her husband was 'prone to disappear'. We called off the search and the old man rolled in three days later with his bike. His only comment was 'I didn't think you'd mind.'

Ken and Maria are very aware of the sense of history on the trails.

I've often felt that we were looking out onto the same countryside as the drivers and firemen of years ago. It's a benevolent feeling.

A family of nine had previously lived in the small house that we had at Middleton Top. They were the Hallows family and one of them remembers lying in bed looking at the icicles on the inside of the window. With the engine house being there you can't forget the railway and all the things that happened there.

The job was a tremendous challenge for Ken.

I knew it would take about a generation for the trails to calm down.

It wasn't only the youngsters who were making a mess of them. There were some quite elderly people who didn't like it being an official countryside site with by-laws and regulations. They weren't used to that. They thought they could pick the flowers – cowslips! – anytime they liked.

To do the job you have to have a certain type of personality. You have to like people, know how to approach them and, slowly but surely, we educated them, explaining why we didn't want the flowers picked. It was difficult for them to realise that while the railway had been there and it was just locals who picked them that wasn't a problem. But the trails were encouraging people in their thousands to come into the area. There was no way they could all pick flowers! We got there in the end but it was a slow process.

And the final word?

I left getting on for nine years ago and the job has changed so much in that time. I can't help thinking I got the best years out of the Countryside Ranger Service.

The end of the railways and the beginning of the trails brought major changes to the villages, some of which brought prosperity to ailing rural areas. But there have been less welcome changes that have altered the characters of the villages to such an extent that some of the people from the old families hardly recognise them.

Hartington hasn't changed all that much in structure. Most of it was built in the seventeenth century and it's been the same ever since but the life of the village is different. It makes its money out of tourism now, catering for walkers and cyclists who use the trails as well as the people from out of town. At one time you could go into The Devonshire and it would be full of locals. All the farmers sat with their dogs under the seat. There was a time when chaps went for a couple

A rights-of-way officer from Cambridgeshire. I'm taking ideas back to my job. If it can be done in Derbyshire we can do it in Cambridgeshire.

Hartington Village

of pints a night, regularly. They can't do that now. The pubs are charging London prices and locals can't afford that.

The community spirit is going, too. People don't know each other like they used to. Some of it's because women are working. It used to be that the women stayed at home, in the village, and they looked out for each other. If a woman had a youngster others in the village would help out. You don't get that now because so many of the houses are empty during the day. You might as well stay at home because you won't find anyone to talk to in the village.

It was laid back years ago. Nobody rushed. It's a myth that all the people in the country had to work so hard. It was hard work in patches. When we were haymaking we'd still be at it at midnight because we had the two hours daylight saving on, but you didn't work like that all the time.

The quarries *were* hard work but not as hard as they like to make out. In the stone yards they'd work like hell for five to six hours a day but that was it and then they'd be off to the pub. Now it seems as if everything is going too fast.

And today's children don't know what it is to be free. We used to wander miles and miles and everybody kept an eye on you as well. You'd get told off by your next-door-neighbour as much as your mum. There'd be hell up if you did that now.

They were safe days. Now it looks idyllic, as if they could just go out and play without anyone worrying, but it isn't like that. We've got the trail and there are a lot of people on it. You want to know where your children are now-a-days. Mothers won't even let their children walk to school. For us one of the bigger kids took us by the hand and dragged us along and when we were older we did the same thing.

People have changed. Years ago they had a zest for life. A bit of something about them. Now it's that dull and dreary. I've never known Hartington so low in my life. There's hundreds of people trailing about but of a night they've all gone. There's just nothing. Plenty of nothing.

This is excellent. It is what we want elsewhere.

There's a real historical feeling to the trails. You can't help but think about those wagons and horses. There's an ambience about it. A good feeling.

In Tissington some things are little different from the beginning of the nineteen-hundreds whilst others have changed beyond recognition.

Tissington still belongs to the FitzHerberts but instead of almost all the villagers working at the Hall there are just one or two that work there now.

There's quite a lot of children in the village but they go to Fenny Bentley school because ours closed down. The old school building is run as a kindergarten by Caroline FitzHerbert from the Hall. She's a teacher by profession. That shows how much things have changed. The FitzHerberts' wouldn't have done that years ago. There's a waiting list for places as the kindergarten but it's expensive, even to go on the list. Most of the children are from outside of the village, doctors' children and the like. I don't think the local people can afford it.

One activity that continues not only at Tissington but throughout Derbyshire is the Dressing of the Wells.

The timing of the dressed wells depends on where Easter falls so it could be very early or as late as May. Work starts on a Saturday and the Well Dressing takes place on Ascension Thursday.

It's a very old craft passed down through generations. About twelve people work together beginning by putting the paper pattern onto the mud. The pattern is pricked round with a dart or something else that is sharp and when the paper comes off the dots are all joined together. We always used alder cones for the outline but now a lot of people use coffee beans; the waste ones from Nestle's. Next come the flowers and leaves. The complete dressing is outlined in yew.

There's a ceremony at each of the wells and a service in Church. It draws very big crowds, coach-loads of people coming from miles away, so the service has to be relayed into the churchyard. All the clergy from outlying villages join in a procession around the village, starting at The Hall Well. Some things never really change.

In the nine years since Ken and Maria Harwood left Middleton Top there have been many changes although perhaps not as obvious as those in the villages. The staff team has grown and the visitors centre has a broader range of goods than would ever have been imagined. The biggest change by far is the role of the Countryside Rangers, although their reasons for joining the service are little different to Ken's. They all have a love of the countryside and an enthusiasm for their work that makes sense of the fact that they all left careers that paid them significantly higher salaries than Rangering ever would.

Andy Pollock, the present Head Ranger, began working for the service in 1981 having trained and worked as a secondary school teacher of Rural Studies.

I came into the job by a very circuitous route. I'm from a mining area to the south of here and I started walking in the National Park because of a teacher at school who enthused about it.

Two years after the track had been ripped up, when I was just sixteen, the site was one of industrial dereliction and a friend and I came to walk the track. We walked on the top of Cromford Moor where the seedlings were less than a metre high. Look at them now!

I taught Rural Studies in Gloucestershire for five years and found it extremely frustrating. I was only getting the environmental message over to a narrow band of children. The kids were important but I wanted to reach more people and I came into the job because of the environmental education side of it. I've never regretted it. I've lived all over the place but Derbyshire was always my spiritual home. I was lucky to be able to come home and take up the job that I'd always dreamed of. I can't think of a patch anywhere that could give more interest, more beauty, than we've got within a ten mile radius of where we work.

I look at the scenery around Tissington and think 'Those guys that were driving the trains were going through this wonderful countryside. They mustn't have thought 'Oh, no, I've got to go to work'.

Views from High Peak Trail

Rick Jillings, Senior Ranger at Middleton Top, has worked on the High Peak Trail for seven years.

After I'd finished my degree in Environmental Science I came back to do voluntary work with the British Trust for Conservation Volunteers in Wirksworth and spent a week up here leading a conservation holiday doing some dry-stone walling.

My countryside work began as a volunteer with the Peak Park Ranger Service before I took a job in countryside work in Essex. Then I came back to Derbyshire. I came back home.

Steve Farren, Senior Estate Warden for the Peak District National Park, echoes Rick and Andy's feelings of identity with his native county.

I came back from working abroad in 1979 and a few years later got a seasonal job with the Peak District National Park supervising volunteers. After a few years my present job was created so I'm the first post-holder and I've been able to mould it the way I've wanted it to go.

I visited the High Peak Trail when it was still a working railway and my father had also worked on the railways so there is a connection. Now I look after three converted railway lines, the High Peak, Tissington and Monsal Trails, and that connection is brought home to me every day. I can see where I was born and all the places I used to cycle to when I was a kid. That's excellent.

The trails have encouraged people to come out into the country. Non-walkers, especially those from the city, can be frightened of the unknown. On the trails they know where they are, they can't go wrong and they feel relaxed and happy.

Robin Jeffcoat has worked in the Derbyshire Countryside Service for ten years having previously been a Mines and Quarries Inspector.

I know this area so well. I used to come up here as a teenager photographing and tape-recording the trains. If you'd said to me then, when I was hurtling around on the back of a motor bike, that I'd end up working here I'd never have believed it.

Herbert Sheppard, Senior Part-time Ranger, sees beginning work with the Countryside Service as a significant point in his life.

I'd been an electrical engineer then went to university to qualify as a teacher and whilst I was there applied for the job of Countryside Warden. There was no pay, just thirty shillings a day retainer, and I worked every other Sunday.

People came into the job for a whole range of reasons and many looked on it as a day out. We worked long hours but we didn't notice the time because we weren't being paid for it anyway. We were doing something we wanted to do and we enjoyed ourselves.

The Countryside Service is often seen as a ghost service – 'What do they do?'- but the recent foot-and-mouth crisis has made the answer clear. People have realised how valuable access to the countryside is to them. To some extent the Trails are taken for granted until they are no longer there but if we want to know whether we are really needed then all we need to do is listen to what the customers said when we re-opened footpaths. They were delighted.

There are changes happening and in the people who visit. Life is much more about acquisition than it used to be. Maybe if we can change our facilities to attract more people then perhaps that'll mean more of them experiencing the range of emotions that we feel about our heritage. I do this job because it is part of my life. It gives me a buzz every time I see the countryside. This is God's country. It is one of the main things that turns me on. Every time I'm out there it's thrill generating whether it's feet deep in snow or I'm looking over the valley and seeing the haze or the Ecclesbourne Valley filled with mist and looking like a fjord. It's all spiritually fulfilling and I can't picture my life without access to these treasures.

Susan Davis is an Information Assistant at Middleton Top who has never regretted her decision to take the job nine years ago.

Views from Tissington Trail

I love it up here. I breathe the air and it's different. It makes me want to take deep breaths.

I studied Archaeology at university and I've become really interested in the Industrial archaeology on the trails. We've been digging out the bottom of Hopton Incline which is part of the old engine house. It served the quarries off the Cromford and High Peak Railway. We've started to uncover a beautiful old wall that looks as if it runs twenty feet down to the bottom. We can't uncover it all because people using the trail might be injured but it is fascinating.

We've had digs where we've invited local people to join us and they've been very popular. Now we've got so many people wanting to join in that we've had to put on another date this year.

It brings a different sort of person to the Trails and I've changed the type of stock that we sell in the shop to reflect that difference. There are a lot of specialists visiting us and we're becoming known as somewhere to find specialist books.

But it's not all about specialisms. Some of the children who visit have never seen the countryside. It's important for them to be able to see and touch. Touch tree trunks, things like that. They really want to learn and want to show us what they've found. It's an opportunity to show them that we can all enjoy the countryside but we all need to take care of it too.

Chris Coombs, Area Countryside Manager, is based at Middleton Top but he began working for the Countryside Service in 1979 as a planner before moving over to work on the trails.

I started as a 'gofer', drawing plans, working out schedules, planting trees. When I qualified I took the next step up the job ladder and, following re-organisation, I became involved in management of the Cromford Canal and the High Peak Trail. At that time the Rangers were answerable to someone else, now I manage both the area and the staff.

There's no doubt we are in a time of change and there's a lot of discussion about how we provide the service, should we provide the service, are we the best people to do it? When the Trails began the job was about looking after the trails and the people who visited them. Full stop. Rangers were Patrol Rangers. Now we simply can't justify paying people to walk up and down the trails. That can't be financially sustained. That doesn't mean that Rangers won't spend time with the public. If they're out working they are accessible and now we have staff such as information assistants who take a more "front line" role with the public. In the 1970's the job could be done by someone who had the enthusiasm and love of the job. Now Rangers are managers, developers of a site. They are involved in contracts partnerships and promoting the use of the rights of way network. They have to have a much wider range of skills and a more professional approach.

A big problem is having to try to do too much. The Countryside Service is expected to do a huge range of tasks from management to maintenance, education to visitor management to interpretation projects and, no matter how good anyone is, no-one can cover that range of subjects and they haven't got the time to do all of those things properly. It mainly falls on the Rangers shoulders but we really need a multi -disciplinary team in order to cope and to be more flexible in how we work.

We used to actively encourage educational parties but we've had to stop promoting the service as we haven't the resources to cope and now we just respond to requests. If we want to continue with the educational side of things then either something else has to be dropped or we find a different way of doing it and what we do is dear to peoples' hearts so it will hurt whatever area is dropped from our work load.

If I go in one of the pubs it could be full but I'd be on my own. A stranger in my own pub.

But change is not necessarily bad. We have to be careful not to get stuck in a rut. The public have different expectations to our visitors in the 1970's. We need to meet those expectations because our fundamental reason to exist is to get people into the countryside so that they can enjoy and understand it. We need to reach the people we aren't reaching because the facilities they want aren't offered or they can't, for some reason, use them.

It all comes down to getting a balance and that's not easy. We've all got our own perception of what is right. But I feel lucky that I do a job that I think is worthwhile and if it's in as good a state when I leave as when I got involved I shall be happy. If it's in an even better state I'll be even happier.

****

So what is it about the job of Ranger that seems to attract and hold people from diverse backgrounds?

The popular, mythical idea of a Ranger is of him striding the hills with his dog and walkie-talkie. And there's such variety in the work. There's the hands-on, practical side of grass cutting and walling; the 'people' side of the job, passing on information, leading guided walks and school parties. We demonstrate the forge at High Peak Junction and manage Cromford Canal which is a site of scientific interest directly connected to the Cromford and High Peak Railway. In recent years the industrial archaeology side of the trails has become very important and that adds yet another dimension to our work. You come to work expecting to do one thing and end up doing something entirely different.

The variety of the job means staff have to be adaptable and have a broad spread of knowledge.

We never forget we are in a privileged position. We can influence so many other people to respect and understand the countryside and to get something positive out of their visits. The breadth of knowledge is very important and so is the local knowledge. We don't only work

Low End, near Hartington

with visitors but with the local land-owners. It's the fact we know to call them 'youth' and to understand when they ask 'Are you nesh, lad?' We know who to call 'duck' and who not to! We know the 'lingo'.

They also need to have an open personality and not mind that the job tends to stretch to twenty-four hours a day.

When you chose to make yourself open to the community you know you'll be approached anywhere, anytime. I can't go to the pub or walk down the street without somebody collars me about something. I've even been given jobs on Ashbourne Market Place on a Saturday morning. And because our job isn't only with the public but with the farmers too we can get a call at ten o'clock at night because they think it's a reasonable time to call or at six-thirty in the morning because they've just finished milking. But that's the part of the job I love, the accessibility to people. They've got somewhere to go if they've got a question about the countryside or they're worried about something that's happening. They can get an answer from us, someone who, hopefully, they can trust. It's like being the village Bobby, teacher or doctor. Not that respect just comes along with the job. We have to earn it.

The work of the Rangers is diverse and interesting. No two days are the same and the flexibility of the Rangers and their broad spread of knowledge are their primary strengths. Their flexibility has made it possible for them to adapt to the many changes that have taken place since the Trails first opened.

Things have changed – some for the good, others for the worse. A big difference is the location of managers. Years ago we didn't have managers on site so the Rangers took more of the day-to-day decisions about what needed doing. Team meetings were held on a Monday, my day off, so I rarely got to see my boss who was based in Matlock. He took the decisions but the actual running of the place was left to us.

THE TRAILS

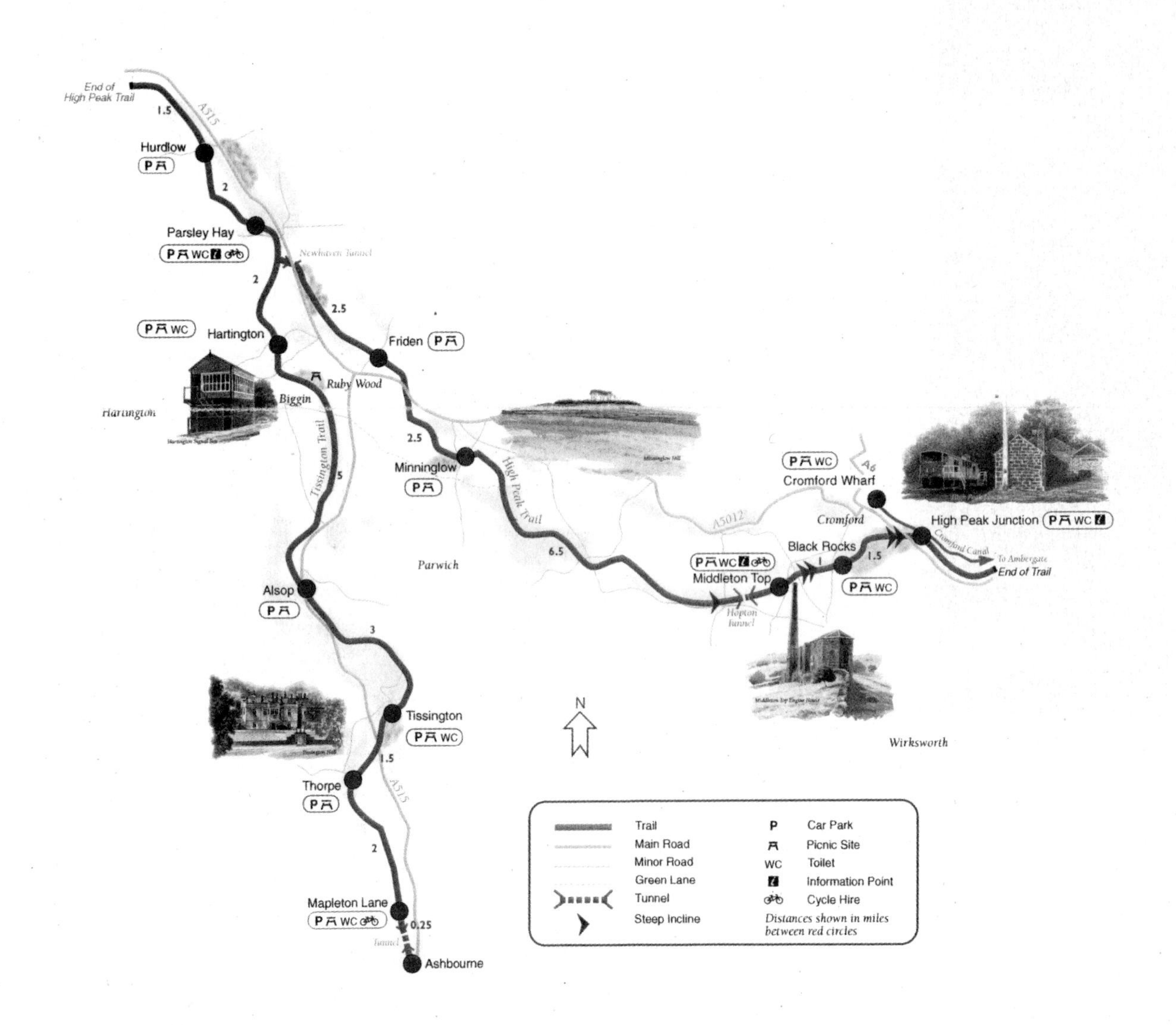

End of High Peak Trail
1.5
A515
Hurdlow
P
2
Parsley Hay
P WC
Newhaven Tunnel
2
2.5
P WC
Hartington
Friden
P
Ruby Wood
Biggin
Hartington
Tissington Trail
2.5
5
Minninglow
P
High Peak Trail
P WC
Cromford Wharf
A6
Cromford
A5012
High Peak Junction
P WC
Cromford Canal
To Ambergate
End of Trail
Black Rocks
1
1.5
6.5
P WC
Middleton Top
P WC
Parwich
Hopton Tunnel
Alsop
P
3
Tissington
P WC
N
Wirksworth
1.5
Thorpe
P
A515
2
Mapleton Lane
P WC
0.25
Tunnel
Ashbourne
Trail
Main Road
Minor Road
Green Lane
Tunnel
Steep Incline
P Car Park
Picnic Site
WC Toilet
Information Point
Cycle Hire
Distances shown in miles between red circles

Cyclist and Horse-Riders on Trail

Many years ago a Ranger said 'The age of patrolling is dead.'

'What's he talking about?' I said. 'Patrolling can't be dead, it plays such an important part in my life.'

Here we are, ten years down the line, and he was perfectly right. We still go out and about but we rarely get the chance to take along a flower identification book and note what flowers we've got or see what birds are around. It would be good just to be able to mingle with the public and say 'It's Sunday afternoon. I'm a Ranger, what can I tell you about the Trail?' It hardly ever happens. But it's good for things to change. We need to keep abreast of what our visitors want and need. Their expectations are different now to what they used to be.

The part-time Rangers who work one day a fortnight used to be called Patrol Rangers but the word Patrol has now been dropped from the title. What they pick up is the work we haven't been able to do in the week so the general public have lost the idea of a Ranger being out there with them. The problem with the system is that we've all got the 'professional eye'. We'd pick things up, notice things. The part-time Rangers can't be expected to do it. They don't have the years of experience and they are only here one day a fortnight.

Quite rightly there's far more thought goes into our work on a formal basis than there used to be - there are far more demands on our limited resources now. We have a Countryside Strategy and work to programmes whereas before we saw the jobs, logged them in our heads and gradually worked through them. We all knew the basis of the job and what needed to be done to make sure it ticked over relatively smoothly.

Now our work is geared to fit in with the different strands of the Strategy; environmental education, access and so on. I feel strongly that environmental education is vitally important and we don't devote sufficient time to it but other than this I feel we have the balance about right.

When I come to the trails I think 'If I were on holiday with my family this would be paradise.'

Brilliant.

Not that the Strategy was pushed onto us. We were sounded out about it and I'm sure that if we had felt we couldn't conform to it or there was something we were violently opposed to, the Strategy makers would have listened to us.

Like many other ventures the Trails have had to be seen to put money back into the pot to ensure their futures. Visitors are the means by which they remain financially solvent and the expectations of visitors have changed.

We've had to become mean and lean and one of the ways we were able to off-set cuts in the bad years was by raising revenue inside the visitors centres. That means selling sweets and souvenirs whether we like it or not.

Visitors are much more sophisticated and have learned to complain if there is something they don't like. We have to follow it up even if there may be little value in spending a great deal of time on it. Many of the visitors have been to places like Alton Towers and seen how well run it is. Whether we like it or not they think the trails are another version and they expect the same standards. I sometimes wonder if people have forgotten what the countryside is meant to be. They seem to want to take something simple and make it complicated.

Other changes are led by the visitors, like the advent of the mountain bike. When they first came out one of the staff who'd been a cyclist since he was a boy, said 'I've never seen anything like it!'
It was a German bike, all terrain. Worth something like three thousand pounds. It was a case of us muttering 'It'll never catch on!'

Within five years we'd gone from a trail that was predominantly used by walkers to Middleton Top in a westwards direction becoming used almost exclusively by cyclists with very few walkers. Some people even call it the cycle track. From Cromford Wharf to High Peak Junction is mainly the domain of the walker and the families. It hasn't been a subtle shift but a major one.

Engine House
at Middleton top

It's hit revenue too because now it's the in-thing to be seen with your own bike. In the past very few people had their own and hired them from our cycle hire centres. We've become victims of our own success in trying to encourage people to see the countryside from a bike.

But the skills needed to be a Ranger remain the bed-rock of the service.

We need to be communicators. We have to be able to talk to adult education groups, university groups, primary kids, the whole gamut of the general public to be able to aim our information. And we have to have a broad knowledge, an appreciation of the different aspects of the trails. Whilst members of the public tend to look at things in isolation we need to see the 'whole'; industrial archaeology, the flora, the recreational potential. It's easy to be enthusiastic about the countryside and we hope this rubs off on our visitors.

Industrial archaeology and the heritage side of the job is becoming more important and many visitors come to the area purely for those aspects of the trails.

The heritage of the trails wasn't really understood when Derbyshire County Council acquired the land but now it is being seen as having value. The historical side is becoming more and more important. The first archaeological dig involved the public and was immensely popular. A spin-off has been an increase in books relating to heritage being stocked in the visitors centre. People now come expecting to find what they want and need.

The engine house attracts lots of visitors every year. They don't necessarily know the history that well but when they see it they can't help but think 'This railway was built in the days when horses were pulling the wagons. Wow.' And they are fascinated.

We've always had specialist visitors to see the beam engine but now we get school parties because what they can see here fits in with the national curriculum. And we've got other things that they want. Anyone out with a group of children needs to know there is somewhere to have their dinner, toilets and a shop where kids with fifty pence or a pound in their pocket can browse. We're providing something for which there is a big market.

Conservation lies at the heart of the Countryside Service and the staff who work on the trails are passionate about their role in ensuring the countryside is there for future generations.

Countryside Services, no matter where they are, are important and need to exist. Last week I visited my Mam in Loscoe on the edge of what used to be a colliery. It's been reclaimed, turned into a playing field and at the bottom there's a stream and a series of old Mill Ponds. I hadn't got a clue what they were when I was a kid but we always called the river 'Red River' because occasionally it ran bright red. That was our nick-name for it and it fitted in well with Cowboys and Indians, Dead Man's Gulch, things like that.

Now a path's been laid and there's an interpretative board: Red River Scheme. It shows why the pond is there, the wild life that live in it, the importance of the little site and that it is being looked after by Loscoe and Heanor Town Council. It made me feel quite emotional. Without some infra-structure to make it better for locals to use, it could have disappeared by now. To me it's precious because I remember it from childhood but now they're explaining to locals why it is a little bit precious and that's exactly what we should be doing.

It's a great shame that the wildlife aspect of the trails has deteriorated. When the trails first started they had been left in perfect condition as wildlife habitats. Now, we don't have the same level of staff as the railway had and in some places the quality of grasslands is deteriorating.

They're ideal for families with youngsters because they are safe and that has to be good. It's safer than them going off into the hills where we have to rush after them if things go wrong.

We balance up the resources to put into the different strands of our job all the time. Some has to go on helping visitors to the site, some to the heritage side and some to conservation management. What we have to do is make sure we can do the job sufficiently well rather than spreading ourselves so thinly that we don't achieve very much.

We've gone a long way since the Trails opened and we've had to sacrifice some things to be able to offer benefits to a wide section of the public. We do get people who don't look after the countryside but the majority come here to enjoy themselves in beautiful surroundings. That gives us the chance to give information that promotes 'greener' ideas and to use the country code to help people understand that we are all responsible for our countryside.

Everyone who works on the Trails has a wish to see them evolve over the coming years to ensure more and more of the public are able to use them. But just what changes might be coming along?

Our trail is a public bridle way and is used by horses and riders but at present we get individuals using the trails or organised events that take place early in the morning before the rest of the visitors arrive. If it is established as a national long-distance route we're likely to see horse-riders using it at all times of day, all times of the year.

When we started the trails we were very much in isolation. Now Tissington Trail is part of the E69 route that starts at Derby Railway Station, runs through Ashbourne and along the trails. We're just the guardians of part of a much longer trail. A lot of these routes were instigated by Sus-Trans, a national cycling charity. They managed to get the tunnel at Ashbourne open. That meant Tissington Trail was linked to Derby. Perhaps the High Peak will one day run again into Buxton. Now that really would be an enormous change.

One of the major ways forward is through the Industrial Archaeology side of the business.

We've only scratched the surface so far. There's a chance Cromford will be awarded World Heritage status which means part of our site would rate on a par with the Pyramids and the Taj Mahal. It won't bring any extra money directly but it will bring a lot of prestige and a lot of visitors. It would raise the profile of industrial archaeology.

It is possible the future might lie in a much more radical idea?

If there is to be a broad look at farming as an industry it may be that farmers are paid not to farm but to look after the landscape and the wild life as well. I don't know if the government would ever go as far as nationalising a certain amount of farmland but if it does it could result in the land almost becoming an integral part of the trails, becoming one entity.

There's a Countryside Stewardship grant scheme that encourages people to look after historic park land and waterside landscapes. In some cases it can be granted for good quality limestone grass lands as well. The farmer is paid to manage the land in a sensitive way.

Or perhaps it is time to think about each bit of this trail being adopted by a farmer or landowner and that they would look after that strip of trail. Many of them have the skills needed and could be given guidance in how to care for the habitat. Maybe it will be a question of looking at what work they've done and working out how much it is worth in monetary terms. Perhaps it would be Rangers who were managing the landowners and farmers. Someone said once 'One day we'll all be park keepers.' He was almost right.

To change things for the future actions have to take place in the present.

If we are going to get the wild flowers to come back we have to think of drastic measures. A lot of the best sites for flowers are the old quarries where there are bare rocks, a bit of a scree slope and over the years we'll get some fantastic flowers growing. But in other areas the

We have to walk circular routes and the trails are great for linking other paths and, as a bonus, the views, especially from the Tissington trail, are magnificent.'

Harry Manley (son of the photographer) cycling the High Peak Trail

soil has become richer and richer. As the vegetation dies back it provides more organic matter in the soil. From bare rock it becomes better quality soil and more grasses, thistles, brambles and nettles appear that simply outshade the wild flowers. This was railway land and it commonly caught fire when the steam engines were going through. The grass was burnt off and the land impoverished, exactly the conditions that wild flowers need to flourish.
We've been saying for years that we need to develop management plans identifying the important species we've got along the trails and carry out a long-term management regime to make sure that the conservation doesn't diminish. But the time spent on that would mean something else didn't get done.

Despite feeling that the wild flowers aren't flourishing as we'd like them to be we do still have a wealth of superb wildlife out there. You can see mile after mile of cowslips, summer wildflowers, ox-eye daisies, vetches. Beautiful.

We're the custodians of this fantastic countryside resource and we want to make sure it is as good as it is now for the next generation.

There was a child who kept asking 'Where does it end?' How do you answer a question like that? How do you explain that it is the towns that end and the countryside that goes on and on?

Ken Harwood

Cowslips were so plentiful that our family used to make wine with them every year.

Cyclists negotiating the notorious Gotham Curve

Railway staff at Sheep Pasture Bottom 1949

© Alan Rimmer Collection

STAFF AT SHEEP PASTURE BOTTOM 1949

	Name	Occupation
1.	John William Spencer	Platelayer
2.	Jim Ward	Wagon Examiner
3.	? Hewson	Goods Agent
4.	Harry Jepson	Joiner
5.	John Willy Porter	Porter
6.	David Wain	Platelayer
7.	Tom Beeson	Hanger-on
8.	Fred Warren	Shed Labourer
9.	Joby Spencer	Number Taker
10.	Major Merrill	Locomotive Superintendent
11.	Fred Hilton	Wigan Wagon Co.
12.	Fred Hurst	Clerk
13.	Geoff Wain	Junior Porter
14.	Hubert Doxey	Fireman Shunter
15.	Harry Bramley	Taker-Off
16.	Steve Bunting	Clerk
17.	Sam Gold	Platelayer

STAFF WORKING ON THE HIGH PEAK RAILWAY DURING 1940'S

Traffic Inspector:	Robert Brunie followed by Jack Smith
Drivers: Middleton Top	Tommy Walker and Harold Kirk
Firemen: Middleton Top	Walter Spencer and Sam Buckley
Cleaners: Middleton Top	Denis Vallance and John Harrison
Guards: Middleton Top	Herbert Slack, George Pearce, Wilf Holmes
Stationary Driver: Middleton Top	Herbert Hallows Snr
Hanger On: Middleton Top	Alec Spencer
Stationary Fireman: Middleton Top	Arthur Gregory
Hanger On and Taker Off: Middleton Bottom	Joe Deakin and Ned Seedhouse
Driver: Sheep Pasture	Jack Harrison
Fireman: Sheep Pasture	Andrew Martin followed by Bill Lowe
Stationary Driver: Sheep Pasture	David Bond
Stationary Fireman: Sheep Pasture	Lionel Brooks
Hanger On:	Sam Hall
Dingle Man:	Cecil Horn
Catch Pit Man:	Herbert Hallows
Hanger On: Sheep Pasture Bottom	Joe Nadin
Taker Off: Sheep Pasture Bottom	Tom Besson
Engine Driver: Cromford	Herbert Kay
Fireman: Cromford	Bernard Walker
Spare Fireman and Shunter: Cromford	Hubert Doxey

© Derbyshire Advertiser/Alan Rimmer Collection

Driver Sam Buckley, Fireman Dennis Vallance and Guard Arthur Millward at Middleton Top before their last turn of duty, 21st April 1967

LINE OF PROMOTION

However much someone wanted to be a train driver there was a set line of promotion in the Motive Power Department. Everyone began as a cleaner and moved on to passed cleaner. Their next step up the ladder was to fireman and on to passed fireman. Only then could they be promoted to driver. At each stage of promotion an Inspector would test staff on their knowledge.

The process of getting from cleaner to driver could take many years. Bernard Walker was fifty-seven years old when he was appointed driver at Cromford.

Payment in the different grades on the Cromford and High Peak Railway was the same as for main line staff but an increase in duties didn't result in an increase in pay. The fireman at Cromford and Sheep Pasture performed shunting and guard duties which saved the company money but he only received the same rate as any other fireman.

THE INCLINE ENGINES

Both Middleton and Sheep Pasture inclines were operated by incline engines. Sheep Pasture incline rose from Cromford Yard and went under the A6 road bridge. In a distance of 1320 yards it went from one inch in nine to one in eight.

The winding engine was built in 1883 and an old locomotive boiler, fired with coal and, later, scrap wood, supplied the engine with steam at eighty pounds per square inch.

Haulage of the wagons was by means of a continuous wire rope that was 2880 yards long. At the foot of the incline there was a large pit that had been built beneath the running tracks and the wire rope passed round it. The rope went underground again at the summit and on into the winding engine house.

When the ascending wagons were in position at the foot of the incline the Hanger On put a tapering chain over the rear draw of the wagon then over the wheels to the front of the vehicle. An implement called a 'donkey', which was about three feet six inches long, was hung on the front draw bar and was slotted at the bottom where a chain was held in position by a nut and bolt.

The purpose of the Donkey was to help keep the ropes in the guide incline pulleys when encountering the curve. Two lighter chains were wrapped around the wagon buffers at the front end and then hooked through the main chain. This helped to pull the rope against the curve pulleys. The Donkey kept the main chain raised and the guide chains were adjusted by the Hanger On to keep the rope on the curve pulley.

The main chain was then plaited round the wire rope and tied by leather throngs. As an extra safety precaution two straps were wound and fastened round the plaited chain.

Descending wagons were attached to the wire rope by the Hanger On at Sheep Pasture Top only at the rear of the wagon.

If two wagons were to descend each one had to be chained separately with a gap between to allow for the slack to be taken up.

The maximum permitted weight of a run, which comprised of two loaded wagons travelling down and three empties coming up, was thirty-eight tons. That gave a balance so that the winding engine was only used to start the balance and for braking.

Signalling on the incline was very primitive but effective and was operated from the bottom of the incline. When the Hanger On was ready to start the run he operated a lever that was connected by wires which rang a bell. There was also a pointer in the engine house with the letter G for 'go' and S for 'stop'. At the top of the incline a semaphore signal coupled to the catch point was operated by the Hanger On which meant that when the points were pulled up the signal showed clear. When the signal was showing danger the catch points were open and set to derail the wagons as a precaution against runaways.

The Taker Off would knock out the scotches that had held the wagons in position whilst they were being hung on to the wire rope and, with points and signals already set, the run started its journey

At Sheep Pasture Top the Taker Off fired the winding engine.

When wagons that were attached to the rope were one-hundred yards away from the catch pit points a bell rang as a signal for the Catch Pit man to pull up the catch pit points, allowing the wagons to reach the incline bottom safely .